TARLA DALAL *India's #1 Cookery Author*

baby
&
Toddler
COOKBOOK

S&C

SANJAY & CO.

MUMBAI

Other Books *by* Tarla Dalal

INDIAN COOKING
Tava Cooking
Rotis & Subzis
Desi Khana
The Complete Gujarati Cookbook
Mithai
Chaat *New*
Achaar aur Parathe *New*

GENERAL COOKING
Exciting Vegetarian Cooking
Party Cooking
Microwave Cooking
Quick & Easy Vegetarian Cooking
Saatvik Khana
Mixer Cookbook
The Pleasures of Vegetarian Cooking
The Delights of Vegetarian Cooking
The Joys of Vegetarian Cooking
Cooking with Kids
Snacks Under 10 Minutes *New*

WESTERN COOKING
The Complete Italian Cookbook *New*
The Chocolate Cookbook
Eggless Desserts
Mocktails & Snacks
Soups & Salads
Mexican Cooking
Easy Gourmet Cooking

TOTAL HEALTH
Low Calorie Healthy Cooking
Pregnancy Cookbook *New*

MINI SERIES
A New World of Idlis & Dosas
Cooking under Ten Minutes
Pizzas and Pasta
Fun Food for Children
Roz Ka Khana
Microwave - Desi Khana *New*

Price Rs. 250/-

First Printing : 2001
Copyright @ Sanjay & Co.
ISBN No.81-86469-57-5

Published & distributed by
SANJAY & COMPANY
353 A-1, Shah & Nahar Industrial Estate, Dhanraj Mill Compound, Lower Parel (W), Mumbai 400 013. INDIA. Tel(91-22) 496 8068
Fax: (91-22) 496 5876
Email: sanjay@tarladalal.com
Website: www.tarladalal.com

Recipe Research & Production Design
Pinky Dixit
Arati Fedane
Jyoti Jain

Nutritionists
Nisha Elchiwala
Punam R. Desai

Design
Satyamangal Rege

Printed by
Jupiter Prints,
Mumbai

Introduction

Motherhood is one of the greatest and most fulfilling gifts bestowed on us by Nature. A flood of tenderness overwhelms you when a tiny, precious bundle of joy is placed into your waiting arms. The birth of your little one will transport you into a new phase of life; one that is both challenging and rewarding. At the same time, there will be a myriad of questions raised in the minds of all new parents! A lot of such questions regarding the weaning and feeding patterns of babies were also directed to me and out of all those queries, germinated this idea of a cookbook for infants and toddlers.

Research has shown that food habits cultivated in the first year of our lives lay the foundation of our eating patterns in the future. Hence, it becomes imperative to begin with a healthy and nutritious diet, one that will hold your baby in good stead throughout life.

Studies have also proved that the eating habits and patterns that are inculcated in babies stay with them for life and also influence their emotional and physical well being throughout their lives.

Most babies today are fed almost anything, right from refined foods, sugar and 'off-the-shelf' baby foods that are readily available and so convenient. Moreover, today's mums usually lack the experienced insight provided by elders, due to the increasing trend of a nuclear family set up. This book hopes to help you deal with a lot of the uncertainties and apprehensions that all new mums face, especially when their babies start weaning.

Writing this book was a very unique experience that has left behind a bundle of memories with me. I am deeply grateful to my dear friend **Dr. Hansa Dalal** and also **Dr. Shashi Merchant**, both of whom are eminent paediatricans. I sincerely thank both of them for sharing their time, knowledge and umpteen experiences which served as an invaluable helping hand in the shaping of this book.

This is a sequel to the Pregnancy Cookbook and lists out delicious recipes for your infants and toddlers from the age of 5 months to the age of 3 years. **These foods are simple and easy to make, wholesome, nutritious and totally baby friendly.**

We have tried to anticipate diet and health related questions that arise in the minds of all new mummies and to provide answers to them. This book hopes to serve as your friend and guide, sharing your pains and joys as you watch your li'l one grow up.

This book has been divided into two main sections—one catering to the needs of infants (from birth to 12 months) and the second catering to the needs of toddlers (from 1 to 3 years). There is also a section devoted to the nutritional needs of breast feeding (lactating) mothers, as it is your diet that will nurture your little one during this period. The section on infancy is further divided into weaning foods for babies in the age groups of 5 to 6 months, 7 to 9 months and 10 to 12 months. There are also interesting recipes for 'foods on the go' and one on 'teething foods' which include quick, easy to make and nutritious recipes.

All the recipes that have been included keeping in mind the nutrient needs of growing babies. Some of these may not really appeal to your taste buds and moreover the textures are also liquid and runny for adult tastes. I can assure you however, that most babies will love them as these have been tested and tasted by a lot of mothers and their toddlers who have added their seal of approval.

My team of nutritionists has carefully analysed each recipe to ensure that they fulfill your baby's nutritional requirements and hopefully satisfy her palate too.

Here I do want to explain that I have referred to the baby as 'she' in this book, not out of any gender bias, but because I was not comfortable with the idea of referring to the baby as 'it'. After all, babies are living, breathing little cherubs and the use of 'he/she' feels too clinical. So I have chosen to call our baby 'she'.

I sincerely hope that this handy book provides answers to all food-related qualms and queries chirping in your mind, whether your baby is a chubby boy or a bonnie lass. But please remember that no book is a substitute for a good paediatrician.

Tarla Dalal

Index

Recipe Index

* Indicates that the recipe is a variation recipe

infancy

(from birth to 12 months)

"Rock - a - bye baby..."

Every time a Baby is born…….. a Mother is born.
Anonymous

Oh! The joys of motherhood.

The immense pleasure on your glowing face as you tenderly croon your little one to sleep will make you realize that the gift of motherhood is the most fulfilling of all.

A baby becomes an inseparable part of the mother and also the entire family by being the harbinger of cheer, happiness and celebrations. As soon as your baby opens her eyes to the outside world, you become the centre of her existence and this tiny precious life becomes totally dependent on you for security, safety and sustenance. You will be amazed at how she trustingly curls her fingers around yours; cherubically innocent in her sleep. This unquestioning trust will fill you with love and tenderness, though not without a trickle of apprehension. This complete dependence may overwhelm you and also make you wonder if and how you feel properly equipped to take on this responsibility. Just sit back and take things easy as this is quite natural and all the moms of the world have had this feeling at some time or another.

These vital first weeks can be nerve racking even if you are totally prepared. Here are some reassuring guidelines to help you sail through these busy months which will be full of mixed emotions of joy, love, insecurity, triumph, anxiety and a whole world of new experiences.

Relax and enjoy these special moments. You are with a friend who will share your joys and worries, provide information and practical knowledge about infants and toddlers including their health, their needs and their nourishment as well.

Have faith in yourself and the special bond that you share with your baby. In times of real doubt, take advice from your paediatrician just as I have and follow that God given **"Mother's Instinct"**.

The birth of your baby will transport you into a new phase of life—one that is both challenging and rewarding. **Take one day at a time and give yourself the opportunity to develop as a parent and to experience the joys of parenting.**

The journey through the nine months of gestation (pregnancy) abounds with miracles as your body miraculously undergoes changes during pregnancy, readying itself for the arrival of your little one. Mother Nature has a wonderful way of preparing you for this special event, both physically and mentally. While still in the womb, your baby will make its presence felt by moving about, as a constant reminder of this wonder. When your baby arrives in this world, she will do so with gusto, crying loudly for you and instinctively clamouring for your milk.

Nature waves her magic wand and most mothers start producing breast milk almost immediately after they deliver. However, for some mothers, this process may take a day or two as your body adapts to hormonal changes. This is quite natural and nothing to worry about. Breast feeding brings its own rewards and like so many aspects of parenthood, it's an art that needs to be learned. To some, it comes easily while others may need more patience.

It's the comfort of being held by you during feeding that strengthens the deep intangible emotional bond between you and your baby. As you cradle your little one closely, this is the closest she can be to the fetal position she's been accustomed to in your womb before birth and so this position provides maximum security for your little one.

Once you start breast feeding (lactating), for the first day or two a yellowish translucent fluid called **colostrum,** is secreted in place of breast milk, that is quite distinct from breast milk. **This fluid is rich in antibodies that build and strengthen your baby's immune system.** Colostrum is also rich in proteins that are vital for your baby's growth and are satiating, thus ensuring that your baby sleeps soundly for longer hours during the first few days. This is nature's way of letting you recover from labour.

Within the next three or four days, this yellowish liquid transforms into **mature milk** which will provide complete nourishment to your baby in the months to come. It is divided into two components— fore milk and hind milk, both of which have specific purposes to serve.

Fore milk, as the name suggests, is secreted at the beginning of the feed and 11 the hind milk towards the end. Fore milk is thinner, rich in protein, lactose, vitamins, minerals, water and low in fat. Fore milk is extremely important as it provides all the above nutrients that are vital for babies at the same time quenching their thirst. Therefore, there is no need to feed any other liquid to your little one for the first four months.

Hind milk is thicker, more opaque and abounds in fat and will satiate baby's hunger. Hence, mother's milk is a complete meal in itself and takes complete care of baby's nourishment. It is important that you allow baby to continue sucking from one breast until she gets to the hind milk and leaves the breast at her own will.

Baby's feed time can be one of the most enjoyable aspects of early parenthood. It is a special time together, inspiring warmth and security, and builds an enduring bond between you and your bundle of joy. In a busy household, it provides you an occasion to relax and also revel in your tiny creation.

For the initial four months, mother's milk serves as the natural self-contained complete food for babies.

Here let me share with you a few wonders of breast milk which makes it a complete food for your baby.

Breast milk is the purest form of nourishment provided by Mother Nature. Providence has provided this source of completely natural nourishment, keeping it at the right temperature for your baby to drink. As breast milk does not demand any pre-preparations in terms of heating and cleaning, the chances of contamination of milk decrease. The chances of overfeeding are also less as your baby will not take more than she needs.

It is rich in antibodies, which increase the immunity in babies, protecting them from cold, cough, influenza etc.

Breast milk contains a protein called lactalbumin and an enzyme called amylase, that aids in digestion and converts the milk into a soft curd that is easily digested by newborns.

A breast fed baby will also have a reduced likelihood of allergic reactions, as the proteins present in the breast milk are less likely to cause allergies.

Lactose is a form of sugar present in breast milk which enhances the absorption of vital nutrients like calcium and magnesium.

Breast milk is easily available for your baby at any time and any place. It is ready to drink and thus the chances of preparing incorrect formula are less.

Apart from this, the action of sucking milk from the breast promotes the development of jaw and facial muscles of your baby.

It has been universally accepted that breast milk is the only complete source of nourishment appropriate for your baby till the age of 4 months. All the nutrients required by your little one are present in the right quantities.

When and how much to feed your Baby

Once your baby has breathed the outside air, her most instinctive and natural action will be to nuzzle your breast and to suck at it. Mother Nature has provided absolutely hygienic nourishment for infants, in the form of breast milk. However, you may be left wondering as to when and how much to feed your little one.

Initially, your baby may not feed at regular intervals. Please don't panic, as this is quite natural. You can feed your baby whenever she cries, irrespective space the day. This natural feeding method is known as **demand feeding.** The important thing is that the baby be allowed to suck at the breast without restriction; she should be able to feed whenever she wants and for as long as she wants.

In the beginning, the interval between two feeds can be approximately 2 ½ to 3 hours as she can consume only small portions. By the end of the second month, the feeding patterns established in the early days can change suddenly and inexplicably. As the days pass, your little one will begin to establish her own routine and will become 'self-scheduling'. She will soon create her own feeding pattern. As her appetite increases, the feeds will get longer and gradually the gap between two feeds will also increase. Simultaneously, your breast milk will also match these new feeding demands. Evolution has provided mothers with the ability to produce as much milk as their baby requires. The feeding pattern will depend entirely upon your baby's needs and here your mother's instinct will hold you in good stead.

The duration of each feed may vary from less than 5 minutes to 20 minutes or more. This will depend upon the flow of breast milk as well as the individual needs of your baby. If the breast milk is flowing adequately, your baby will be satisfied soon. If not, she may take a little longer, especially if she decides to take a snooze in the middle of a feed.

Try not to fix any rigid timing or follow a regimental, artificially systematized timing to feed your baby as there is no place for clock watching here.

Once your newborn starts feeding, she will close her eyes blissfully switching off visual signs and will submerge herself totally in the comfort of your arms and taste the rewards of feeding. When she is satiated, she will usually push the nipple out of her mouth and gurgle merrily. This infantile gesture will clearly indicate that your baby is no longer hungry.

Proper positioning of your baby will also help to enhance feeding. Snuggle your little one close to you with her chin skimming your breast and the rest of her body facing you. Make yourself comfortable, put on some soft music if it helps you relax and feed your baby in a calm and relaxed atmosphere as stress and anxiety may decrease the production of milk. Your vulnerable little one is extremely sensitive to the environment. She can feel your stress and this will also affect her feeding.

It is important to feed your baby from both the breasts. Your baby, if left to her own resources, will never want to leave the security of your arms and will enjoy being stuck to your bosom indefinitely. Most paediatricians recommend that once your baby has adjusted to breast feeding, she should be fed for 20 minutes at each breast, as this will also be more comfortable for you. If you are constantly feeding from one breast, the other one will remain heavy.

Burp your 'precious', once half way through the feed and then again after the feed is over. This helps to release any wind that has been swallowed by baby during feeding or crying. However, if your baby falls asleep while feeding, do not disturb her slumber. Put her on her side and not on her stomach or back and gently pat her back to allow the wind to escape. Some milk may also run out of baby's mouth with this burp. This is normal and there is no need to worry about it, unless the baby looks uncomfortable. Wipe it off with a clean napkin and continue feeding, if you are half way through the feed.

Sometimes babies burp on their own during the feed and this is also a sign that baby has had her fill. It is not necessary to burp the baby again, in such a situation.

Alternatives to Breast Feeding

Sometimes large amounts of milk are produced two or three days after delivery but it may also take a while for your baby to get used to sucking and her efforts may cause sore nipples, preventing you from nursing. You may also be recovering from surgery and not in a position to breast feed immediately.

At such times, you can still feed baby breast milk by expressing the milk and refrigerating it till it is required. Breast milk can be safely stored for 4 to 6 hours at room temperature and for upto 24 hours, if refrigerated. It is imperative to pay meticulous attention to hygiene. Always remember to warm the milk in a sterilised container before feeding it to your baby.

If you do find it difficult to breast feed your little one initially, try and be patient and do not give up easily. The way to make breast feeding a success is to continue to breast feed, as the production of milk in the breasts is dependent upon the amount your baby feeds. Paediatricians recommend breast milk as their first choice because it contains valuable antibodies that strengthen baby's delicate immune system.

In case you do need to start substitutes like top milk (milk of cow or buffalo) or powdered milk, consult your paediatrician as he will know what's best for your baby. These substitutes will also take care of your baby's nutrient requirements just as breast milk.

Cow's milk is an ideal substitute as its nutritional quality is very close to that of mother's milk. However, research shows that the protein content of cow's milk is triple the amount in breast milk and such high proteins are not required for your baby at this age. *So, if you choose cow's milk, then it is important to dilute three parts of this milk with one part of sterilised water.* Buffalo's milk, on the other hand, has a higher fat content and may be difficult for your little one to digest in the early months.

Powdered milk formulas should be given second priority, as the chances of over and under dilution are higher as compared to cow's or buffalo's milk. *If you choose to start on formula milk, follow the instructions given on the package accurately.* If you feel the need to make any changes in the dilution instructions, do so only under the guidance of your paediatrician. Remember to sterilise all the containers that will be used to prepare formula and to feed your baby. Also ensure that sterilised water is used to dilute formula milk.

While preparing a feed for your baby, one objective needs to be top most on mind to provide a safe, easily digestible, hygienic and nutritious feed for this precious life. Whether you choose cow's milk or buffalo's milk, boiling the milk prior to feeding is essential and will ensure safe and micro-organism free milk for your baby. If the milk is refrigerated, you will need to warm it to room temperature. It is always safe to check the temperature of the milk by pouring a few drops of milk on your wrist or the back of your palm to ensure that it is tepid. Also, check for the quality of milk by tasting it. If it tastes sour, discard it immediately as it may be harmful for your little one.

Do not be anxious or feel guilty if, for some reason, you cannot breast feed your baby, as this may only be a temporary phase. It is important to remember that your baby's future is shaped more by good parenting and less by the kind of milk you choose.

Lactose Intolerance

Biologically speaking, it is most natural for a baby to be fed on mother's milk or a similar substitute. However, some mums may spend agonizing moments wondering why their little one vomits or has loose motions after she has had milk, while the baby next door happily gurgles down milk.

Lactose is a form of sugar present in milk, which is broken down into simple sugars with the help of an enzyme called lactase that is produced by our bodies when we consume milk. Some babies may produce lactase in insufficient quantities and therefore are unable to digest milk. This is commonly known as lactose intolerance.

A deficiency of this enzyme may cause an inability to digest milk, due to which some infants may develop colic, get diarrhoea or even start vomiting on consuming milk.

Some babies may be able to digest dairy products like curds and paneer only to a certain extent when they are older. Others may tolerate milk when mixed with other foods. If your baby is not able to digest milk at all, then you need to consult a paediatrician who is the best guardian of your baby's health. He will keep in mind your baby's special needs and will recommend other substitutes like soya milk or groundnut milk which have a different type of sugar and are easier to digest.

However, lactose intolerance could be a temporary phase as the body produces lactase only as and when it is required i.e. when one consumes milk. Be attentive in such a situation and consult your paediatrician.

Mother's Diet during Lactation

A newborn baby radiates irresistible appeal and can transform even the most sophisticated parents into doting protectors. You will obviously always be anxious and careful about your li'l one's health. This protective instinct will urge you to pay great attention to your own diet, especially while you are breast feeding. Your baby depends totally on you for sustenance, especially during the first 4 months after birth.

Your breast milk is dependent upon the quality of food and quantity of fluids you consume. This, in turn, will directly affect your baby's nourishment and well being. Hence, you need to follow a sensible diet, one that includes vital food elements and keeps you both healthy and well.

Most paediatricians recommend breast feeding infants for a year, out of which the first four months the baby should be exclusively breast fed and then gradually weaned over the next 6 to 8 months. If you decide to follow the same pattern, here is what you need to supplement your diet with during lactation. All the nutrients below have been calculated for mothers with moderate activity levels.

1. While you are lactating, your **energy** requirements will increase to enable you to keep your strength up. All food groups provide energy, which is expressed in technical terms as kilocalories or what we commonly refer to as calories. *One point I would like to explain here, is the relation between calories (cal) and kilocalories (kcal). They represent the same values and are referred to by two different names i.e. calories and kilocalories.*

You will actually need to consume at least **2400 to 2700 kcal every day during first 6 months of lactation.** At this time, the energy requirements of your body are higher as you will be exclusively breast feeding your baby. However, in the latter 6 months, when you start weaning by introducing variety in your baby's diet, you will breast feed less frequently and so your energy requirements will decrease to **2250 to 2550 kcal per day.**

Lactation draws on your energy resources and burns **3500 kcal per day.** You do realize that you will actually be burning more calories than you are consuming. Are you quizzical about the source of these extra calories? Hidden here is another miracle of nature. This will be the time to use maternal stores that you have accumulated during your pregnancy. Mother Nature will go about "Her work", helping you to shed those extra kilos you may have gained during pregnancy. This is the time for getting back into shape naturally, provided you eat wisely.

I remember being forced to eat laddoos and panjiri loaded with ghee when I was breast feeding. Your mother, in her love and concern for you, may advice and entice you into eating these traditional goodies. Indulge yourself, but do remember that moderation is the key word and ghee provides no real nutrition to you or your baby except vitamin A and energy. Also, it will make you put on weight.

So supplement your diet with plenty of wholesome foods like
✤ Cereals such as wheat, rice, bajra etc.
✤ Dals and pulses such as moong dal, rajma, soyabean etc.
✤ Dairy products like milk, pasteurized cheese, paneer, curds etc.
✤ Fruits, vegetables and their juices

2. While you are lactating, you will need to consume more **protein** too. The requirement is approximately **70 to 75 gm per day during the first 6 months of lactation.** As you supplement breast milk with weaning foods your protein requirement should also decrease a little by 5 to 7 gm i.e. to about **63 to 70 gm per day.**

Make the following protein rich foods a part of your diet
✤ Dals such as moong dal, toovar dal, masoor dal etc.
✤ Pulses like rajma, chawli, chana etc.
✤ Dairy products like milk, pasteurized cheese, paneer, curds etc.
✤ Nuts and oilseeds (almonds, cashewnuts, til, groundnuts etc.)
✤ In particular, soyabeans and its products such as tofu, soya nuggets etc. are considered to be an excellent source of vegetarian protein

3. **Fat** is a concentrated source of energy and **45 gm per day** of it is required while you're lactating. This moderate amount of fat is required to supplement your maternal stores to achieve optimal secretion of breast milk.

4. As your breast milk is the only source of nourishment for your little one in the initial months, your body will continuously be using up some of the most important **minerals and vitamins** and these resources will require replenishment.

You will need **3800 mcg of vitamin A (Beta Carotene) per day** during the lactation period. Vitamin A is vital for the immunity as well as the glowing skin and clear vision of both you and your little one.

Have plenty of
✤ Dark green leafy vegetables such as amaranth, spinach, fenugreek etc.
✤ Yellow orange fruits and vegetables like carrots, pumpkin, tomatoes, papaya etc.
✤ Dairy products like milk, pasteurized cheese, paneer, curds etc.

5. Vitamin C is one of the most important nutrients, keeping colds and coughs at bay by strengthening immunities of both mummies and babies. So your need for vitamin C doubles during lactation to about **80 mg per day.**

Good sources of vitamin C are
✤ Citrus fruits like orange, guava, lemon, sweet lime etc.
✤ Vegetables such as capsicum, cabbage, broccoli and coriander
✤ Other foods like papaya, tomato, amla etc.

Amla is a gold mine of vitamin C and one small amla per day fulfils your daily requirement for this nutrient. Vitamin C is highly unstable and is lost during cooking except in the case of amla which retains most of its potential even after being cooked.

6. Calcium is one of the most vital minerals essential for the development of your baby's bones and teeth. During lactation you will need to consume **1000 mg of calcium per day**. Breast milk is a good source of calcium.

A word of caution here; the calcium levels in breast milk are not affected even if your diet lacks in calcium rich foods, but in such a situation breast milk unfortunately, derives its calcium from your bones, making them weak. This may lead to deficiencies later in life and can lead to osteoporosis.

Make the following foods an essential part of your diet
✤ Dairy products like milk, pasteurized cheese, paneer, curds, etc.
✤ Dark green leafy vegetables such as spinach, fenugreek etc.
✤ Soyabean and its products such as tofu, soya nuggets etc.
✤ Til (sesame seeds) and ragi (nachni)

7. Iron is an essential component of haemoglobin that supplies oxygen to each cell of our body. Although **breast milk** is a poor source of iron does not provide substantial amount of iron to your baby, you require iron **(30 mg per day)** to maintain your haemoglobin levels.

To make up for your iron requirements, consume

✤ Dark green leafy vegetables such as spinach, cow pea leaves, fenugreek etc.
✤ Nuts such as almonds, cashewnuts etc. and oilseeds such as til and garden cress (subza) seeds
✤ Dried fruits like raisins, dates etc.
✤ Whole grain cereals and pulses such as bajra, cow peas, dried peas etc.
✤ Jaggery

8. **Folic acid** plays a major role in multiplication and formation of new cells in our body. To prevent folic acid anaemia, you need to consume **150 mcg of folic acid per day.**

Increase your folic acid levels by enjoying

✤ Vegetables such as cluster beans, spinach, peas, broccoli, beetroot, ladies finger, potato (especially unpeeled) etc.
✤ Cereals like bajra, wheat and pulses like soyabean, rajma etc.
✤ Nuts like almonds, cashewnuts, walnuts etc. and oilseeds such as til

9. **Vitamin B$_{12}$ (1.5 mcg per day)** is essential for proper functioning of all cells in our body. In comparison to non-vegetarian foods, vegetarian diets are deficient in vitamin B$_{12}$. But don't let that dampen your spirits as soya and its products such as soya milk, soya nuggets etc. in particular provide appreciable amounts of this vitamin.

10. **Vitamin D** is also an important nutrient which aids the absorption of calcium. It is synthesized in our body in the presence of sunlight. Hence, there is no dietary recommendation for this nutrient in our tropical weather.

11. In addition to the above nutrients, you must also include foods like almonds, fenugreek (methi), garlic, milk and garden cress (subza) seeds etc. to stimulate the production of breast milk. These foods are called galactogogues and they enhance the production of breast milk.

12. **A liberal intake of fluids is equally important as the production of breast milk is largely dependent on the amount of fluid you consume daily.**

Have at least 4 litres (or **more** but **not less**) of fluid daily during lactation including plenty of juices, soups, dals, buttermilk etc. This will help to enhance breast milk production and also maintain the fluid balance in your body.

Recommended Dietary Allowance for Infants and Toddlers

Along with the dietary requirements for mothers the **Indian Council of Medical Research (ICMR)** has also suggested the Recommended Dietary Allowance (RDA) for infants and toddlers. The table below list all the major nutrients required for their healthy growth.

Recommended Dietary Allowance (RDA) for Infants and Toddlers per day.

Nutrients	0 to 6 months	6 to 12 months	1 to 3 years
Energy	108 kcal/kg	98 kcal/kg	1240 kcal
Protein	2.05 gm/kg	1.65 gm/kg	22 gm
Fat	✤	♣	25 gm
Calcium	500 mg	500 mg	400 mg
Iron	1 mg/kg ✤✤	1 mg/kg	12 mg
Vitamin A	1200 mcg	1200 mcg	1600 mcg
Vitamin C (Ascorbic acid)	25 mg	25 mg	40 mg
Vitamin D	200 to 400 IU	200 to 400 IU	200 IU
Vitamin B_1 (Thiamin)	55 mcg/kg	50 mcg/kg	0.6 mg
Vitamin B_2 (Riboflavin)	65 mcg/kg	60 mcg/kg	0.7 mg
Vitamin B_3 (Niacin)	710 mcg/kg	650 mcg/kg	8.0 mg
Vitamin B_6 (Pyridoxine)	0.1 mg	0.4 mg	0.9 mg
Vitamin B_{12} (Cyanocobalamin)	0.2 mcg	0.2 mcg	0.2 to 1.0 mcg
Folic Acid	25 mcg	25 mcg	30 mcg
Vitamin E	5 IU	5 IU	✤✤✤

✤ Although ICMR has not made any specific recommendations for the consumption of fat for babies, it is essential in moderation for the healthy growth and development of your baby.

✤✤ Breast milk is a poor source of iron. However babies are born with adequate iron stores which suffice their requirements for the first 4 months. Therefore, the requirement for this nutrient begins only after

✦✦✦ After the age of 1 year, there is **no** specific recommendation for vitamin E as most of the foods we **consume** like cereals, pulses, fruits and vegetables contain plenty of vitamin E.

Major Nutrients and their Importance

Listed below are the important **nutrients** essential for infants and toddlers, along with their **functions** and the **food sources** that will provide these nutrients.

NUTRIENTS	IMPORTANT FUNCTIONS	SOURCES
Energy	✤ Healthy growth and Development ✤ Required for our daily activities	✤ Cereals such as wheat, rice, bajra etc. ✤ Dals and pulses such as moong dal, rajma, soyabean etc. ✤ Dairy products like milk, curds, paneer etc. ✤ Fruits, vegetables and their juices
Protein	✤ Skeletal as well as muscular growth and development ✤ Maintenance and repair of cells	✤ Dals and pulses such as moong dal, rajma, soyabean etc. ✤ Dairy products such as milk, curds, paneer etc. ✤ Soyabean and its products such as tofu, soya nuggets, soya milk etc.
Carbohydrates	✤ Extremely necessary to provide heat and energy to the body	✤ Whole grains and their products like whole wheat, rice, pasta, whole wheat bread etc. ✤ Vegetables like potato, yam etc. ✤ Fruits like banana, chickoo etc.
Fat	✤ Serves as a concentrated source of energy ✤ Carrier of fat-soluble vitamins like vitamin A, D, E and K ✤ Healthy development of brain	✤ Visible fats and oils like sunflower oil, soyabean oil, corn oil, peanut oil, vanaspati, butter etc. ✤ Invisible fats which as the name suggests is the hidden fat present in all foodstuffs like nuts, oilseeds, cereals etc.
Calcium	✤ Formation and strengthening of bones and teeth	✤ Dairy products such as milk, curds, paneer, etc. ✤ Dark green leafy vegetables such as broccoli, spinach, fenugreek etc. ✤ Soyabean and its products such as tofu, soya nuggets, soya milk etc. ✤ Til (sesame seeds) and ragi (nachni)

Continued...

NUTRIENTS	IMPORTANT FUNCTIONS	SOURCES
Iron	♣ Essential for the formation of haemoglobin, which supplies oxygen to all the cells in our body. ♣ Production of red blood cells	♣ Dark green leafy vegetables such as spinach, cow pea leaves, fenugreek etc. ♣ Nuts such as almonds, cashewnuts etc. and oilseeds such as sesame seeds (til), and garden cress (subza) seeds ♣ Dried fruits like raisins, dates etc. ♣ Whole grain cereals and pulses such as bajra, cow peas (chawli), dry peas etc. ♣ Jaggery
Zinc	♣ Overall growth and development ♣ Promotes brain development	♣ Whole grains like bajra, ragi, wheat etc. ♣ Pulses like whole Bengal gram, cow peas, soyabean etc.
Vitamin A	♣ Required for healthy skin ♣ Normal process of growth and vision ♣ Strengthening of tooth enamel ♣ Increases immunity and provides protection from diseases	♣ Dark green leafy vegetables such as fenugreek, spinach etc. ♣ Yellow orange fruits and vegetables like carrots, pumpkin, tomatoes, papaya etc. ♣ Dairy products like milk, curds, paneer etc.
Vitamin B_1 (Thiamin)	♣ Helps in providing energy and for nerve metabolism	♣ Cereals such as wheat, wheat bran, rice, rice bran, jowar etc. ♣ Leafy vegetables like fenugreek, spinach etc.
Vitamin B_2 (Riboflavin)	♣ Promotes healthy skin ♣ Helps in providing energy, protein, carbohydrates and fat	♣ Dairy products such as milk, curds, paneer etc. ♣ Green leafy vegetables such as cow pea leaves, colocasia, spinach etc. ♣ Cereals such as wheat, rice, bajra etc. ♣ Dals and pulses such as moong dal, rajma, soyabean etc.
Vitamin B_3 (Niacin)	♣ Helps in the metabolism of protein, carbohydrates and fat and supplies energy	♣ Whole cereals such as barley, wheat, rice bran etc. ♣ Dals and pulses like chana dal, soyabean, moong etc. ♣ Groundnuts

Continued...

NUTRIENTS	IMPORTANT FUNCTIONS	SOURCES
Vitamin B_6 (Pyridoxine)	✤ Helps in the breakdown of protein and fat	✤ Cereals such as wheat, jowar etc. ✤ Vegetables like broccoli, potato etc.
Vitamin B_{12} (Cyanocobalamin)	✤ Required for proper functioning of all cells in the body	✤ Soyabean and its products like soya nuggets, tofu etc. are the only vegetarian source of this vitamin
Folic Acid	✤ Multiplication and formation of new cells	✤ Vegetables such as cluster beans, soyabean, spinach, peas, broccoli, beetroot, ladies finger, potato (especially with the skin on) etc. ✤ Cereals like bajra, wheat etc. and pulses like soyabean, rajma etc. ✤ Nuts like almonds, cashewnuts, walnuts etc. and oilseeds such as til
Vitamin C (Ascorbic acid)	✤ Strengthens your baby's immunity and protects her from infections ✤ Promotes development of teeth, skin, muscles, bones and cartilage ✤ Aids in the absorption of iron present in the food	✤ Citrus fruits like orange, guava, lemon, sweet lime etc. ✤ Other fruits like amla and papaya ✤ Vegetables such as broccoli, capsicum, coriander and cabbage
Vitamin D	✤ Aids in the utilization of calcium in the body which in turn makes the bones healthy	✤ Can be manufactured by our body in the presence of sunlight ✤ Milk and eggs
Vitamin E	✤ Essential for maintaining healthy cells ✤ Healthy maintenance of skin	✤ Vegetable oils like corn oil, safflower oil etc. ✤ Cereal grains like wheat, wheat germ, bajra, jowar etc. ✤ Dark green leafy vegetables like spinach, fenugreek etc.

Discover the secret

to healthy living,

Discover

Bertolli Olive Oil.

Olive Oil is a pure vegetable extract that comes from ripe olives. It has been used since ancient times for general well-being and finds multi usage as wide ranging as edible oil to massage oil. It brings to food a balance of calories, vitamins (A, F) and antiradicalic agents proportional to the individual need.

A pure and healthy product, it contains the highest level of monounsaturated (good) fat among all vegetable oils. Studies have shown that it helps in reducing cholesterol. Further more, antioxidants such as vitamin E, vitamin K and polyphenols are also found in Olive oil, which are known to prevent cancer and atherosclerosis, as well as reduce blood pressure.

A COMPARISON OF COOKING FATS*

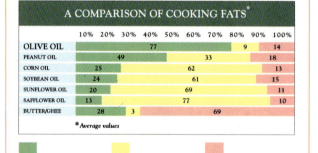

Oil	Monounsaturated Fat	Polyunsaturated Fat	Saturated Fat
OLIVE OIL	77	9	14
PEANUT OIL	49	33	18
CORN OIL	25	62	13
SOYBEAN OIL	24	61	15
SUNFLOWER OIL	20	69	11
SAFFLOWER OIL	13	77	10
BUTTER/GHEE	28	3	69

*Average values

Monounsaturated Fat
- protects "good" cholesterol (HDL), reducing the level of "Bad" cholesterol (LDL)
- reduces the risk of heart disease and diabetes

Polyunsaturated Fat
- reduces the level of both "good" (HDL) and "bad" (LDL) cholesterol
- oxidises readily
- breaks down into potentially toxic substances during cooking

Saturated Fat
- increases levels of "bad" (LDL) cholesterol
- increases the risk of cardiovascular disease

As shown above, using Olive oil (with its higher MUFA base) is healthier than using higher PUFA based oils such as Sunflower oil or Safflower (Kardi) oil.

Olive oil and childhood

Diet is fundamental in childhood. Lipids have a particularly important role to play and lipid requirements are greater in childhood than adulthood. Recommended ratio of 4:3:1 between saturates, monounsaturates and polyunsaturates should be observed in the infant diet which is similar to that of human milk since all fatty acids are needed to build the child's biological membrane.

Olive oil has a good ratio between saturated and monounsaturated fatty acids, is highly digestible and contains essential fatty acids. Therefore, it can be considered a proper food for infants from their 4th-5th month. Olive oil provides essential fatty acids for the development of neonate, besides which its omega 6:omega 3 ratio is similar to that of human milk.

Experiments have proved that the best skeleton growth and mineralization were obtained on intake of oleic glycerides supplemented by a minimum amount of polyunsaturated fatty acids (which is what is normally found in Olive oil). The high level of oleic acid in Olive oil (55 - 83%) helps in bone growth in infants.

The use of Olive oil in weaning foods is ideal for its optimal ratio of linoleic and alpha-linoleic acid. Its very high content of monounsaturated oleic acid is very important for bone mineralization and brain development.

Infants and children require a diet in which there is a predominance of monounsaturates and polyunsaturates accounting for 8-10% of total calorie intake. These recommendations are ideally met in the composition of Olive oil.

weaning
(from 5 to 12 months)

Your baby will enjoy the best of health on a diet formed exclusively of breast milk until she is 4 months old. Once past this age, she will have increased needs for certain nutrients that can no longer be met solely through breast milk. Also this is the time to start introducing new foods and textures to your baby's diet. This supplementary feeding (feeding in addition to breast milk) needs to be introduced gradually. **It is a transitional stage where your baby's diet gradually changes from one of breast milk alone to one based on what you and your family eat. This is called WEANING.**

As your baby grows older, you may worry about the "right" time to introduce your little one to weaning foods. Your baby is the best person to help you out of this dilemma. She will show telltale signs like putting a toy or finger in her mouth or demanding feeds at shorter intervals or be restless during the night. She may also show some interest in other kinds of foods apart from milk. **Most paediatricians recommend that weaning foods be introduced by the end of 4 months. However, let your baby guide you as to when she is ready for these supplementary foods.**

The right age for weaning and introducing such supplementary foods to your baby's diet is end of the 4th month or beginning of the 5th month. About this age, your baby will begin to show signs of learning new feeding skills. This may then become the ideal time to acquaint your baby with newer textures and tastes too. Prior to this age, your baby's delicate digestive system may find it difficult to cope with anything other than milk. Hence most paediatricians are not in favour of early weaning.

Weaning is not about charts or time. Weaning is about readiness. So, a gradual shift from breast milk to supplementary feeds is always advised.

We have divided weaning into 3 stages, each of which has progressive changes in the diet, that will vary with each baby depending on personal preferences, growth and development (teething) and your baby's ability to adapt.

What to start with?

Weaning is a period of experiments, both for you and your baby. It is really a matter of trial and error to find out what is best for your baby. Most paediatricians advise weaning gradually over a period of time beginning with home cooked foods using fresh ingredients as these are healthy and easily digestible for your little one.

When you initiate your baby to weaning, the question uppermost in your mind will be — *"What and how much to start with?"* Well, the answer to this one is simple.

Start with anything that is healthy and easily digestible and let your baby guide you about the quantity she is ready for. It is usual to start with half to one teaspoon of a mashed cereal like rice or even fruit or vegetable juice initially and to gradually increase the quantity to about half a cup. Both liquid and semi-solid supplements can be introduced to your baby's diet at 5 months. Start with one or two additional feeds each day during the first month of weaning. Gradually, as the number of supplementary feeds increase, the interval between breast feeds will also increase.

Your little one may really enjoy this treat and begin to show signs of savouring the first taste of real food. However, it is also possible that she may take some time getting used to newer foods. Some babies adapt to weaning quicker while others may be fussy for a while before they adjust. You will have to be patient during this period.

Introduce your baby to weaning gradually and lovingly, making it a pleasurable experience both for you and your precious one. Do not force your baby to eat foods she does not want to eat. It is not unusual for babies to react badly or be allergic to some foods, so watch your baby's reactions closely when you introduce a new food.

The best time to introduce supplementary foods is during the daytime, when your baby is fresh and also hungry. If she is not hungry, she will not accept any new food and may even become cranky. So, feeding during the day will save both you and your little one an uncomfortable night as digestion is easier earlier during the day than in the latter half.

Start by offering one food at a time and continue this for a couple of days before trying something new. This way, if your baby does have an adverse reaction to a particular food, you will know the likely culprit. It is recommended that you feed your baby yourself till she is one year old. This will give you exclusive personal time with your little one and strengthen the maternal bond of love. This is the most important time for nurturing your precious one. You will soon be adept at feeding your baby and this time spent together will be precious for both of you.

Always hold your baby comfortably on your lap in an upright position while feeding. This will make swallowing easier for your baby and also prevent choking on foods. A small, rounded spoon with a long handle is the safest means to feed your baby as it will not injure her mouth or gums. Put a small portion of food on the spoon and gently place it on your baby's tongue. If she likes it, you will hear a swallow and if not, you'll see a splatter!

Weaning Foods

There are varying opinions about the sequence of weaning foods. Most babies are accustomed to a diet composed entirely of milk till the fourth month. So initially, it is a good idea to introduce weaning with liquid supplements like soups, juices and dal water starting from the fifth month onwards. These can be followed by semi-solid supplements like mashed cereals, fruits and vegetables. **You should begin with 1 to 2 such supplementary feeds every day, preferably, in the morning. Later, you can add one more feed in the evening.** Consult your paediatrician before you start weaning, as he will be the best person to guide you about the special needs of your baby.

Liquid Supplements

1. Milk

It is usually extremely difficult and impractical to continue to exclusively breast feed your baby beyond 4 to 6 months. However, if you feel comfortable nursing beyond 1 year, feel free to do so. But do remember to start additional foods at the appropriate time because research shows that babies who are weaned later have a harder time adjusting to weaning.

By the fifth month, your baby's digestive system will have become stronger and you can safely start on undiluted milk, if you're not breast feeding and your baby is on diluted cow's or buffalo's milk.

This will also be the right time to reduce the number of breast feeds and substitute them with fresh milk (cow's or buffalo's) gradually. Do remember to boil the milk before giving it to your baby. This will not only destroy the disease causing bacteria but also soften the proteins present in it, making digestion easier. Most mothers prefer to start feeding milk using a training cup or a spoon instead of a bottle. **Start with a few teaspoons at a time and slowly increase to about half a cup.**

2. Fruit and Vegetable Juices

A well-balanced diet is essential, especially during these initial months of weaning. Your little one is growing now and will need vitamins and minerals to make her strong. Fresh fruits and vegetable juices of carrots, oranges, sweet limes, muskmelon etc. which are storehouses of vitamins B and C as well as iron are the best foods to supplement a milk diet.

Straining these juices is necessary to make digestion easier. However, most paediatricians recommend that fruits like custard apple, pineapple, gr apes, watermelon and guavas should be avoided till your baby is one year old.

To begin with, introduce your baby to a single fruit or vegetable juice at a time. This will help you to identify your baby's likes, dislikes and allergies, if any.

Follow this with a combination of 2 to 3 fruits or vegetables, once baby has adjusted to a single fruit. Try Papaya and Muskmelon Juice, page 57, after baby is six months old and has adjusted to both the fruits individually. **Start with one teaspoon and gradually increase the amount to about half a cup per day.**

Sometimes, your baby will screw her face and spit out some juice. It is possiblethat she may not like the tangy taste of citrus fruit juices. Try juices purées of non-acidic fruits like muskmelon, banana, chickoo etc.

It is better to avoid mushy vegetable juices like tomatoes as they may Contain some indigestible shreds even after you strain them and these may be difficult for your baby to digest, especially till she is 6 months old.

Before you start preparing your baby's meal, do remember to wash and sterilise all the utensils and equipment you use.

Stay away from myths and superstitions. A prevalent notion that fruit juices must be warmed before feeding to prevent your baby from catching a cold is completely erroneous. Warming or heating will destroy the volatile vitamin C present in them.

3. Vegetable Soups and Dal Water

Strained dal water is the best one to begin with, especially moong dal as it is easier to digest. Serve Moong Dal Water, page 56, and see on your little one's face light up. You can also begin with thin strained vegetable soups such as carrot, pumpkin, bottle gourd etc. These are a good source of iron, calcium and vitamin C. As your baby grows older and is about 7 months old, you can start on unstrained soups and dals.

It is advisable to begin with one type of vegetable soup or dal and gradually accustom your baby to a combination of these vegetables and dals. Try vegetable variations like Beet and Carrot Soup, page 58. A wide variety of soups and dals will help your baby savour and develop a palate for foods other than milk.

Semi-Solid Supplements

Babies are most likely to take to semi-solid foods with gusto, savouring this addition to their regular diet of milk, soups and juices. It is also quite possible that they may resist these changes, resulting in a messy meal and splattered clothing and furniture. Do not be alarmed by this as your baby may resist new tastes initially. It is a natural process where she is trying to adapt to new foods and to learn the skill of swallowing foods other than liquids while also adapting to newer flavours.

It is not essential to follow a strict drill or order in which to introduce the supplementary foods. However, the best semi-solid supplement for your baby initially, is a single cereal, pulse or a mashed fruit or vegetable.

Rice is the most common cereal to begin with as it is nutritious and easiest for babies to digest. Gradually, try a combination of a cereal and pulse, such as rice with moong dal in the form of khichdi. Your baby would best accept a well mashed khichdi thinned down with warm water, which will be easier for her to swallow and digest. Serve Moong Dal Khichdi, page 54, and watch your baby happily gurgle it down.

Other cereals such as wheat, ragi, bulgur wheat etc. can be added once your baby starts accepting semi-solid foods. Cook these cereals with milk to give a smooth creamy consistency that is balmy for your baby's tongue. Add a teaspoon or two of butter or ghee to these foods, as they are a rich source of energy. A great start can be made with Bajra Porridge, page 65, which is an unusual and yummy porridge to initiate your baby to this diet. Begin with one to two teaspoons and gradually increase the quantity to about half a cup.

To meet the increased demands of calories and protein of your growing baby, you can also start with **malted porridges** that are made with different grains like wheat, ragi, bajra, jowar etc. The process of malting involves soaking the grains overnight, draining the water and tying them in a muslin cloth to allow them to sprout for 2 days. Finally, dry roast the grains on a tava and then grind into a flour. This process converts the starch present in these grains to amylose due to the increased production of an enzyme called amylase and hence it gets the name **Amylase Rich Food (ARF). This conversion makes thinner porridge and enables your baby to eat more.**

Flip the pages and try Malted Magic, page 65. This is great to carry with you if you are going to be travelling with your baby as it makes a nutritious and hygienic meal for your little one. You can also add these flours to baby's milk shakes, soups and dals to make her meals more nutritious. Once your baby accepts these changes, it is time to introduce her to mashed fruits and mashed dals as well. Most babies will love the sweet taste of fruits and will welcome this innovation in their regular diet. A mashed banana (diluted with a little milk) makes an excellent meal. Chickoo, papaya and ripe mango can also be great additions. Introduce stewed fruits like apples a week or two later.

By the end of the fifth month, most babies readily accept more variety and can be served boiled and completely mashed vegetables like carrots, potatoes etc. Ensure that these vegetables are properly cooked and blended to a semi-solid consistency so that they are easy to swallow.
Remember to begin with a single fruit or vegetable and gradually introduce your baby to combinations.

Food Square

The perfect weaning foods for your baby should consist of a combination of staple foods, protein supplements, fruits and vegetables for vitamins and minerals and sugar, fats and oils in moderation.

The Food Square below will help you to understand the basic food groups and their combinations that form a balanced diet that is the basis of supplementary feeding.

All the components of the Food Square are important to nourish your baby. However, it is not necessary to provide for all these either in the same meal or at the same time. Introduce your baby to these foods graduallly, letting her adjust to their taste beginning from the fifth month onwards.

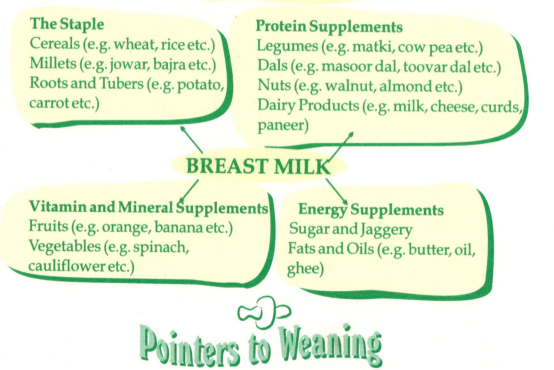

FOOD SQUARE

The Staple
Cereals (e.g. wheat, rice etc.)
Millets (e.g. jowar, bajra etc.)
Roots and Tubers (e.g. potato, carrot etc.)

Protein Supplements
Legumes (e.g. matki, cow pea etc.)
Dals (e.g. masoor dal, toovar dal etc.)
Nuts (e.g. walnut, almond etc.)
Dairy Products (e.g. milk, cheese, curds, paneer)

BREAST MILK

Vitamin and Mineral Supplements
Fruits (e.g. orange, banana etc.)
Vegetables (e.g. spinach, cauliflower etc.)

Energy Supplements
Sugar and Jaggery
Fats and Oils (e.g. butter, oil, ghee)

Pointers to Weaning

✔ Weaning is a period of experiments, both for you and your baby. It is really a matter of trial and error to find out what your baby really likes as most babies show strong preferences, even at this early age.

✔ Wean your baby gradually over a period of months. Your little one is less likely to be distressed when weaning happens gradually.

✔ During the initial days of weaning, allow your baby to lick on some foods, preferably liquids, so that she gets accustomed to different kinds of flavours and textures. When you start on semi-solid foods, start with foods that are very thin in consistency like Apple Punch, page 57. You will need to add sterilised water or milk to thin down the consistency, if required. As your baby gets accustomed to thinner foods, you can gradually thicken the consistency. Along with this, most babies are ready for a mashed cereal or fruit. Encourage your baby to wean by providing other nourishment like Masoor Dal Water, page 56, or Banana Smoothie, page 63, in place of breast feeds. Your baby will need plenty of loving attention while you both make the transition from nursing to weaning. She will be your best guide during the initial period of weaning and she is the only person whose opinion on this subject counts.

✔ While introducing any foods for the first time, watch out for any allergic reactions like cough, cold or skin rashes. If these occur, discontinue that food immediately and consult your paediatrician.

✔ Sometimes she may dislike some foods so much that she may just throw them back at you. At these times, avoid giving the same food a second try immediately. Wait for a few weeks before you try again. In the meantime, you can also offer her another food to introduce her taste buds to new flavours. However, if your baby continues to dislike that particular food, try and add an accepted food to a rejected one to get your baby used to the taste gradually.

✔ Feed your baby in an upright position. This will make swallowing easier and will prevent her from choking on foods.

✔ Try not to show any sort of dislike towards any food while feeding your baby as babies are good imitators and get influenced very easily.

✔ It is always better to be guided by your baby's appetite than to feel pressured into overfeeding her. Do not urge your baby to eat more than she wants. Instead, try and understand her expression towards food. Learn the pattern of your baby's feeding requirements from her body language. Some babies show signs of hunger by waving their hands or kicking their legs when they see food. While other babies may lean forward and open their mouth or cry loudly. When they are no longer hungry, they will reject food by turning their mouths away or spitting it out.

✔ Most doctors are of the opinion that babies do not have a discerning palate for sugar and salt until the age of 7 months. It is wiser to avoid adding them to your baby's meals as a sweet tooth is usually cultivated rather than inherited. If your baby develops a taste for sugary foods at this age, this in turn may lead to dental problems and obesity later in life. Dried fruits like dates and figs or honey or jaggery can be used as alternative sweeteners. Be sure to use fresh honey as stocked up honey may contain micro-organisms which can be harmful to your baby.

✔ Avoid adding strong spices like pepper and garlic to your baby's meals at least till she is 6 months old as she may find them unpleasant to taste and may reject foods containing these spices.

✔ Babies generally accept lukewarm foods more readily. Avoid serving hot foods to your baby. Always bring the temperature of the food down to lukewarm and check it by feeling it on your palm or wrist.

✔ It may seem tough initially and you're both going to throw your share of tantrums at meal times, but try and be patient and resourceful.

✔ If your little one is sick, consult your paediatrician about changes in her diet.

Seven to Nine months

Your *precious one* will be a continuous source of pride and joy to you and will continue to win the hearts of your family and loved ones with her heart warming antics. She will have begun to recognize familiar faces and will start responding to you and making overtures by the time she is 6 months or a little older.

By now your little one is not so 'little' any more, weighing approximately twice as much as her birth weight. In addition to breast feeding, your baby now needs **2 to 3 supplementary feeds daily**, preferably one in the morning, a second one in the afternoon and the third in the evening.

She will also have got used to the liquid and semi-solid supplements in her diet. Most babies are at their active best at this age and may also establish a fairly regular eating pattern. You will need to pay special attention to her diet to provide nourishment for all her activities over the next 3 months. Your baby will need all her energies and so will you!

At this stage, your baby will welcome new textures in her diet like finely chopped and cooked vegetables, whole cooked dals, unstrained soups and juices. You can start reducing the number of breast feeds by introducing juices and liquids to your baby's diet.

Your little one may drool and be irritable at times and chances are that she's teething. Give your baby finger foods like a small piece of toast or carrot, peeled and de-seeded tomatoes or peeled cucumber to nibble. These will help soothe your baby's gum irritation. Your baby may also start showing signs of independence and will want to hold on to foods. Check out other teething foods such as Teething Biscuits, page 81, Whole Wheat Bread Sticks, page 79 etc. These foods encourage your baby to be independent and also give her an opportunity to savour different tastes and textures. Supervise carefully while your baby is chewing on such foods as she can gulp a big piece down and may choke on it.

This is also a great opportunity for her to start learning eating techniques like biting and chewing. As your baby starts cutting teeth, she will want to nibble on anything that comes in her way. She may be irritable and refuse food, wanting to bite on hard objects. This is the time when you have to be careful and alert to take care not to keep any sharp objects within your baby's reach as they can hurt her.

During the teething months, sometimes babies may show signs of indigestion or vomit out their food. This is usually a result of chewing on all kinds of things to ease gum irritation. Sterilise all the toys that your baby is likely to chew on. Be careful that your baby does not eat any uncovered food to relieve her irritation, as it may be unhygienic and cause digestive problems like diarrhoea and dysentery. Please do not panic and do consult your paediatrician at such times.

You can also now start adding more flavours to your baby's food. Temper her meals with subtle spices and condiments like salt, pepper and herbs so that she develops a taste for them. Some babies may just love this addition to their meals and happily consume spicy foods like onion, garlic after 6 months while others may find even a simple carrot indigestible. Introduce spices to your baby's meals only gradually. Add a regulated quantity of iodised salt to your baby's meals, as iodine is extremely essential for the functioning of the thyroid gland which controls the metabolism of our bodies and lack of iodine leads to hormonal irregularities.

Changes in Weaning Foods

The food groups will remain the same as they were in the last phase viz. 5 to 6 months. Only the textures will change and now you can introduce a larger variety of foods to your little one's diet.

As your baby grows older, around the age of 8 to 9 months, you can introduce whole wheat bread, whole wheat pasta and also dairy products other than milk like curds, buttermilk, paneer etc.

Liquid Supplements

1. Milk and Other Dairy Products

Your little one may have already become accustomed to the new foods in her meals so you can now decrease the number of breast feeds and increase the fresh milk from ½ cup to about 1 cup per day to replace breast milk. This is also an ideal time to start with home-made milk shakes, porridge diluted with milk, paneer (cottage cheese) etc. to add good sources of calcium to your baby's diet. Try Chickoo Milk Shake, page 68, or Fruity Phirnee, page 69, which are good combinations of milk and fruits and will definitely please your little one.

2. Fruit and Vegetable Juices and Soups

By the age of 7 months, most babies begin to experiment with the techniques of biting and chewing and they are quite ready for **unstrained soups and juices** in increased quantity. All the vegetables, especially green leafy vegetables, can be cooked in small amounts of water and blended along with the water that it is cooked with, as this is rich in water-soluble vitamins like B and C. To minimize the risk of infections, do remember to wash and peel the fruits and vegetables thoroughly before feeding your baby.

Semi-Solid and Solid Supplements

Although your baby may be eating the same foods as before, their consistency will change as she will have acquired new skills like biting and chewing. She may have already graduated to eating mashed cereals (porridge), mashed fruits and vegetables and will be ready to try something adventurous. Grab this opportunity! This is the right time to different combinations and textures of food to your baby's diet.

Gradually, start with cooked whole dals and pulses as alternative sources of protein to supplement your baby's diet. Well-cooked dals such as toovar dal masoor dal, moong dal and vegetables can be served at this stage. Add a teaspoon of butter or ghee to improve their nutritive quality, as babies need plenty of nourishment to help them grow.

Your baby may also be able to handle a moderate amount of spices in her diet by now. So, do perk her meals with a simple tadka (tempering) of jeera (cumin seeds) and hing (asafoetida) as these are therapeutic and also aid in digestion.

Food Groups and their Combinations

Make your little one's meals innovative and interesting. Use different combinations of foods, as shown in the table below, to introduce a variety of textures to your baby's diet and make it energy and nutrient rich.

FOOD GROUP	EXAMPLES	SUGGESTED RECIPE
2 Food Group Combination	Cereal + Pulse	Moong Dal Khichdi, page 54
	Cereal + Vegetable	Spinach Pasta Puree, page 74
	Milk + Fruit	Fruity Cream Cheese, page 72
3 Food Group Combination	Cereal + Fruit + Milk	Fruity Phirnee, page 69
	Cereal + Vegetable + Milk	Palak Paneer Rice, page 76
	Cereal + Vegetable + Pulse	Vegetable Khichdi, page 77

While introducing these foods to your baby's diet, begin with a 2 food group combination and gradually move on to a 3 food group combination. Do not introduce more than one food group combination to your baby. If she does not accept a particular combination, do not worry. Wait patiently for 2 to 3 weeks and re-introduce the same food again. In the meanwhile, try other food group combinations instead.

Time will fly by and before you even realize it, you will be getting set to celebrate your baby's first birthday. By now, in addition to breast milk, **4 to 5 supplementary feeds per day** are necessary for your growing baby.

There are no hard and fast rules about when your baby should progress from one stage to the next. However, usually most babies adjust to semi-solid and solid supplements with real gusto by the tenth month. Moreover, as they approach their first birthday, they begin to show interest in eating all those foods that other family members around them are eating and they are willing to experiment with them. **This is the best time to gradually accustom your baby to eat with the family and also to eat the same meals as the family does.** Try and eat at least one family meal every day with your baby.

These meal times are also a good way for her to learn to feed herself and encourage her to be independent. She will learn to eat quicker and be more motivated to be self-sufficient by watching others at the table. Give her a spoon to eat on her own and serve food cut into tiny 'bite-sized' pieces so she can handle it easily. You can fill the spoon for your baby, but leave the actual feeding to her. Even if it is slightly messy in the beginning, she will soon learn her table manners.

Weaning Foods—Changing Textures

Like most adults, babies also eat with their eyes first, so their meals should look appealing. Make her meals more appealing by including colourful fruits and vegetables like carrots, beetroot, tomatoes, oranges etc. Cut her food into different shapes and sizes so that the food looks fascinating. Meal times should be a happy time for you and your little one.

Liquid Supplements

1. Milk and Other Dairy Products

By the 9th or the 10th month, most mothers are in the process of giving up breast feeding. This is the time to increase the quantity of fresh milk to replace the breast milk. At this age, babies need to have at least 2 to 2 ½ cups of milk everyday, whether it's breast milk or top milk. Growing babies need a constant supply of calcium and protein in their diet to help their bones and teeth to grow and strengthen. Along with milk, this is also a good time to introduce cheese to your baby's diet to supplement the calcium requirement and at the same time acquaint her with a newer taste and texture. If your little one is fussy about milk, try giving milk shakes, curds, cheese, paneer and even home-made ice-cream to supplement protein and calcium in her diet. Recipes like Spring Vegetable Risotto, page 93, and Strawberry Yoghurt, page 63, serve as good sources of calcium in your baby's diet.

2. Fruit and Vegetable Juices and Soups

You can continue to serve unstrained vegetable soups and fruit juices as appetizers before meals or in the evenings. Fruit juices are great sources of a natural sugar called *fructose* that provides instant energy to keep your baby perked up. This will also take care of your baby's hunger until meal times. Most paediatricians are against giving juices and soups during meal times, as they can affect your baby's appetite and she may not be so willing to eat her meal after that. Again, do remember that there are no hard and fast rules and if your baby is happier with a 'soupy' dinner like Dal and Vegetable Soup, page 94, just go ahead with it.

Semi-Solid and Solid Supplements

This is a period of transition and exploration for your baby; especially where her diet is concerned. She is most likely to be ready for a switch from mashed foods to finely chopped and lumpy foods. However, some babies are reluctant to accept this transition and may just be really happy gulping mashed foods. Include a variety of chopped vegetables like carrot, potatoes, spinach etc. to your baby's meal. Your little one is going to be extremely attracted to colourful and '*feel-good*' dishes so do pay attention to the colour and texture of her meals. Colourful dishes like Vegetable Parathas, page 88, Corn Sambar, page 96, and Dal and Rice with Grated Cabbage, page 90, will be easily accepted by your baby at this stage.

As your baby grows older and starts teething, encourage her to have whole fruits and vegetables like banana, chickoo, apple, carrot, cucumber etc. These will also soothe her gums if she is teething. Also, chewing food is a great exercise for your baby's gums when she is teething and helps to strengthen the new teeth that are emerging. Peel and cut the foods into bite-sized pieces. Fruits and vegetables provide bulk in the diet and aid in baby's bowel movements too.

The good news for you is that you may no longer need to prepare special meals for your baby. By the end of the first year, your baby can start eating everything from your family pot. Just keep her portion aside before adding spices and seasoning to the food for the other family members. **In fact, a wonderful way to acquaint your baby with your 'ghar ka khana' is to mix 1 or 2 spoons of your regular food to the portion you've kept aside for her. This will gradually help your little one adjust her palate to these new and wonderful tastes of your home cooking.**

At this age, you can also introduce fermented foods to your baby's diet, as these are nourishing and easy for your baby to digest. Curds is an example of a fermented food that is commonly eaten on a daily basis. However curds is introduced into your baby's diet at about 5 months because its easier to digest. Idlis, dosas, dhoklas etc. made with a combination of a cereal and pulse are also good examples of fermented foods which can be added to your baby's diet from the 10th month onwards. Vegetable Idlis, page 95, is a fermented dish which your baby will definitely relish! Some foods like whole nuts, raw peas, corn etc. should be avoided till your baby is 1 year old as they can cause choking. For that reason, they're not safe for your baby to eat at this stage in their whole form. However, as they are nutritious, you can mash or purée them before giving them to your baby. Peanut Brittle, page 116, Corn Sambar, page 96, etc. are a few examples of such foods.

Six to Twelve months

Developing Healthy Eating Patterns during Weaning

Around the sixth month, when weaning is established, most mothers complain that their babies are fussy about eating. I think all you budding mummies out there need to know a little secret; that your little cherubic angel can be a real devil at 'khana time' (meal times).

Yes, babies do throw tantrums at meal times mostly because they are being forced to eat when they are not hungry or they are being fed what they don't like. Do not despair as this is usually a passing phase and a minor compromise can bring about an amicable truce. Give baby one food that she likes along with a food that she does not much care for. **A sensibly planned yet flexible pattern of feeding will form the basis of good eating habits, that will stay with your little ones for a lifetime. Small babies are amazingly adventurous in their tastes if you give them an opportunity and if you experiment with their meals.** So add variety to your baby's diet as it is the key to stimulate a sense of enjoyment and anticipation around meal times. Bright colours, fancy shapes and different textures are the ladder to stimulate your baby's appetite. For example, a raita of carrots and beetroot in curds will be much more appealing than a bowl of plain curds. It is wiser to keep proportions small initially so as not to overwhelm your baby and then to gradually increase the portion size.

Establish a feeding routine and try to feed the baby at the same time each day. Tying a bib around baby's neck is a sure signal that it's feeding time. Babies who are able to sit on a chair can be given a spoon or a bowl to play with while you are preparing to serve them. They sometimes like a companion to share their meals with. Try a favourite toy, teddy bear or a doll.
Babies should be encouraged to be independent from a young age. Therefore as soon as they start grabbing a spoon, allow them to have one. Trying to copy you is common, so allow your baby to feed you or the teddy bear and do not worry about the mess. Meal times will certainly be less messy as baby gets more practice. It's important to stay relaxed and avoid making a fuss.

If you feed your baby a monotonous diet, eating will soon become boring and a chore and make your baby suspicious about tasting new and unfamiliar foods. These food habits will stay with your baby for a long time, as tastes developed early in childhood tend to stay into adult life too. studies have also shown that the eating habits and patterns which are inculcated in babies stay with them for life and also influence their emotional and physical well-being throughout their lives.

Frequent and untimely snacks during playtime should also be discouraged as it leads to unhealthy eating habits and can ruin her appetite for meals. **Avoid bribing your baby into eating, as babies don't understand that concept. So don't let them learn it so early in life.** Try to avoid tempting your baby to eat in front of the television. Encourage her to eat with other family members or play sit down games during meal times.
Avoid junk food and processed foods as they can make your baby agitated

or hyper as a result of the additives and preservatives present in such foods.

Try not to get your baby used to fried or refined foods. Too many sweet treats like laddoos, cakes or sugary cookies are also unhealthy for your little ones. Cater to your little one's sweet tooth by encouraging healthier nibbles from the very beginning. Dried fruit purées, small pieces of raw fruits, low sugar cookies, thin bread sticks, steamed vegetables are all good choices. Try recipes like Whole Wheat Date Cookies, page 82, Apricot and Fig Purée, page 62, Fruits with Custard, page 97, Jowar Bajra Bread Sticks, page 80, etc.

It is always better to feed your baby family meals that are home-cooked, but snacks like wafers or chocolates should be allowed in moderation because if children are deprived completely, they can develop an unhealthy craving for them later in life.

toddlerhood

(from 1 to 3 years)

As your little one gets ready to celebrate her 1st birthday, stepping into the fascinating world of toddlerhood, she will be about three times (triple) her birth weight.

The stage from her first birthday until she starts school, i.e. **from 1 to 3 years is the stage of toddlerhood.** These are the crucial years for laying the foundation of your baby's health. Most babies outgrow the stage of eating mashed and bland foods and will now begin to eat more elaborate meals. They are now ready to eat everything that is being cooked for the other family members.

Do remember that the food habits formed at this age will hold them good for a lifetime. So you need to ensure that she eats healthy and nutritious food. Encourage your toddler to eat whatever she likes and treat her palate to a variety of foods so that she cultivates a taste for new foods and flavours.

For you, this stage can be a magical experience, as you will see your baby gaining independence and ability very rapidly. Between the ages of 1 and 3 years, your bundle of energy will grow very rapidly, learning to crawl, talk etc. During this period, she will need to be fed more frequently. Unfortunately, right now, her small stomach is not in a situation to cope with large meals. **So, offer small and frequent meals to your child.**

Also remember not to set hard and fast rules in terms of a particular time or number of meals, because what is really important is not the number of times your child eats but what she eats. **You need to emphasize on the quality and not quantity of food she eats.** Be flexible, as rigidity regarding meal times may lead only to stubbornness.

Most babies show a decrease in appetite during this year, as they are busy concentrating on learning other skills. If your baby is one amongst them, do not worry as babies usually eat whatever they like and demand food whenever they are hungry.

They may get tired, cry or nibble on anything that's within their reach. Now you need to be more attentive than usual, as your little angel may not understand that she is hungry and will probably realize it only once food is in sight. If she is hungry, she can cry or throw a tantrum too, so you need to be alert and remind her to eat by offering her food at regular intervals.

It is possible that sometimes she may refuse to eat for no apparent reason. In your loving efforts to ensure that your baby eats a good balanced diet, remember that the coin is in your child's hand, too. *If you insist on force feeding, meal times will soon become a tug of war between you and your child, making her extremely unpleasant and also making your toddler develop an aversion to food.* If your little one is **not particularly** interested in all the foods that you offer and chooses to eat **one or two** things, do not force her to eat the foods she does not wish to eat. **She will surely make up for this** lack of eating in her next meal. Mothers are **agonized if** their baby has had no milk for one day, but it's okay to take a **break from** regular everyday foods once in a while. Tempt her with cheese or **paneer** instead.

Some toddlers are also **fussy about** what they like and what they want to eat. By now, they have strong **preferences** which might make you want to tear your hair out sometimes. **This situation** can be handled if you follow the basic principle of serving your baby the foods that she is already accustomed to and enjoys **while** continuing to add new foods to her diet. Fussing over her may **convey that** eating is a means of getting family attention.

Cook dishes that your **toddler** enjoys. Also it is wiser to mask foods she doesn't like by mashing **or puréeing** it. You can also mix those ingredients with your toddler's favourite ones. For example, if your baby does not like carrots, try giving her Carrot Cake, page 114, instead.

Toddlers also like variety in terms of textures, shapes and flavours as their taste buds are now almost developed.

Daily Food Guide for Toddlers

The best indicator that your toddler is getting adequate nourishment is regular weight gain, growth, general appearance and contentment.

Thinking of which foods **are healthier** for your baby will be much easier for you by now, as you will be **an expert** on which foods your child is best able to cope with. All the food **groups** viz. cereals, pulses, fruits, vegetables and milk are equally important and are extremely healthy for your child.

An adequate amount of **these** food groups will ensure a healthy growing child. Very few of us really **know** what is the adequate intake for our little toddlers. **The Daily Food Guide** overleaf will help you to know the right amount of food that your child should consume at this age.

Daily Food Guide for Toddlers

FOOD GROUPS	No.of Servings per day	What makes 1 serving	Suggested Recipes
CEREALS AND THEIR FLOURS Whole wheat, unpolished rice, jowar, bajra, ragi (nachni), bulgur wheat (dalia), corn, whole wheat pasta, whole wheat bread etc.	5 to 6 servings	1 slice of whole wheat bread (25gm)* or 2 phulkas (30 gm)* or 1 chapati (25 gm)* or ½ cup all cooked cereals and pasta (60 to 80 gm)*	Whole Wheat Bread (page 111) Jowar Bajra Rotis with Paneer (page 101) Sprouts Khichdi (page 102) Spinach Pasta Purée (page 74)
PULSES **Whole** Moong, lobhia beans, rajma, chick peas (kabuli chana), etc. **Sprouts** Moong, rajma, matki etc. **Dals** Moong dal, toovar (arhar) dal, masoor dal, chana dal, urad dal etc. **Flours** Moong dal flour, chana dal flour (besan) etc.	1 to 2 servings	¼ cup raw whole pulses (35 to 40 gm)* or ½ cup cooked whole pulses (70 to 80 gm)* or ½ cup of raw or cooked dals (70 to 80 gm)* or ½ cup of flours (40 to 60 gm)*	Rajma Salad (page 104) Moong Sprouts Dosa (page 108) Dal and Rice with Grated Cabbage (page 90) Teething Biscuits (page 81)
VEGETABLES Carrot, beetroot, cucumber, brinjal, french beans, cluster beans (gavarfali), cauliflower florets etc. **Leafy Vegetables** Spinach (palak), fenugreek (methi), lettuce, radish leaves, coriander, cow pea (chawli) leaves, colocasia, cabbage etc.	2 to 3 servings	½ cup raw vegetables (50 to 70 gm)* or ½ cup cooked vegetables (50 to 70 gm)* or 1 cup raw leafy vegetables (15 gm of vegetables like mint, coriander, fenugreek and 40 to 60 gm of other leafy vegetables)* or ½ cup cooked leafy vegetables (15 gm of vegetables like mint, coriander, fenugreek and 40 to 60 gm of other leafy vegetables)*	Paneer and Vegetable Parathas (page 100) Beetroot and Carrot Raita (page 103) Coriander Curd Rice (page 75) Dal and Vegetable Soup (page 94)
FRUITS Pineapple, sweet lime, orange, guava, watermelon, mango, apple, etc. **Dried fruits** Almonds, cashewnuts, walnuts, sesame seeds (til), peanuts, dates, figs, apricots etc.	2 servings	½ cup chopped fruits (50 to 60 gm)* or 1 big piece of fruit e.g. melon wedge (100 to 130 gm)* or 1 cup fruit juice (200 ml)* or ¼ cup dried fruits (20 to 30 gm)*	Yummy Apple Porridge (page 71) Fruity Chana Salad (page 104) Muskmelon and Watermelon Juice (page 99) Whole Wheat Date Cookies (page 82)

46

Continued..

DAIRY PRODUCTS Milk, curds, paneer, pasteurized cheese etc.	2 servings	1 cup milk (200 ml)* or 1 cup curds (200 ml)* or ¼ cup chopped paneer (35 gm)* or ¼ cup grated cheese (35 gm)*	Chickoo Milk Shake (page 68) Strawberry Yoghurt (page 63) Fig and Apricot Cream Cheese (page 73) Cheesy Corn and Vegetable Cutlets (page 113)
FATS AND SUGAR Ghee, oil, butter, sugar and jaggery	**	Although there is no specific recommendation for this group, approximately 2 tablespoons of fat and 2 to 3 teaspoons of refined sugar can be consumed per day	Jowar Banana Sheera (page 70) Vegetable Parathas (page 88) Carrot Cake (page 114) Spiced Walnut Ring (page 115)

* The weights of all the foods mentioned in the above table are approximate values.

** Fats should be consumed in moderation as some foods like walnuts, sesame seeds and even cereals contain invisible fat which are also a part of our diet. Excessive fat can disturb the absorption of important nutrient like calcium in your little one's body, apart from increasing the risk of obesity later in life.

Do remember that it is not necessary to provide all these nutrients to your child in a single meal. They can be part of a snack, a complementary dish like raita, or even a teething food.

Include at least one nutritious protein rich dish in each main meal (i.e. lunch and dinner) e.g. Paneer and Vegetable Parathas, page 100.
Although milk is an extremely good source of protein, most toddlers are fussy about drinking it. Add variety with a milk shake or her favourite mix like Horlicks or Maltova. You can also supplement your child's diet with other dairy products like paneer (cottage cheese), cheese, curds (yoghurt) and homemade ice-creams occasionally. *Two glasses of milk are a must every day in any form to provide for their daily requirements of protein as well as calcium.* Cheesy Corn and Vegetable Cutlets, page 113, is a healthy way to incorporate not only cheese but also vegetables in your child's diet.

As cereals form the maximum number of servings, try and serve whole cereals like whole wheat, rice, bajra, jowar etc. [avoiding maida, semolina (rava) etc.]. These cereals can be served throughout the day as in-between snacks. Since your toddler will need to eat more frequently, remember that cereals are good sources of energy and hence are important for your little one. Jowar Bajra Rotis with Panner, page 101, and Carrot Cake, page 114, are healthy choices.

for your child at this age. Include a **variety of** fruits and vegetables as a major part of your child's diet. These **raw foods** not only add colour but also aid in your child's bowel movements **due to their** high fibre content. I know that most children are fussy about **eating fruits** and vegetables but they will enjoy them if they are presented **attractively and** cooked in a way they like. Introduce different cooking methods **like baking**, roasting, sautéing etc. and new food combinations just as **you had d**one during the first year of your baby's life. If your toddler is **fussy about** fruits, try a fruit shake or a tart filled with fruits or Fruity Phirnee, **page** 69, or Fruits with Custard, page 97. For vegetable fussy toddlers, **disguise** them in dishes like Dal and Rice with Grated Cabbage, page 90, **or Spring** Vegetable Risotto, page 93. You can also try and combine cereals **with veg**etables or fruits with milk while cooking meals for your child. **These combinations** will help you to improve the palatability of foods which **in turn** will encourage your child to eat more too. Check out our healthy **combinations** like Fruity Chana Salad, page 104, and Beetroot and Carrot Raita, **page** 103.

You can also add some spices and **condiments** like salt, turmeric powder and a dash of chilli powder to enhance the taste, colour, flavour and appeal of the food.

Handy Tips to make Meal Times Fun and Healthy for your Toddler

1. **Children are good imitators.** So set a good example for them by eating a variety of foods yourself. Always offer a variety of foods to ensure that your child is getting a balanced diet. Try not to show any dislike towards specific foods while feeding as your child may easily be influenced by you.

2. **Try and serve small amounts of food at each meal and encourage your child to have a second serving if she wants to.** Make meal times pleasant and allow your baby to eat what she wants to eat. Being rigid with her food will only make her stubborn. Be flexible but firm.

3. **Encourage your child to have at least one meal with the family members.** This is also a good time to encourage your child to feed herself if she hasn't started already. Do not expect anything other than a messy meal time in the beginning. Very soon, she will master the art of eating on her own with good table manners, making you a proud mum.

4. **Ensure that your child sits upright and is not lying, running or playing**

while eating. You could also engage her in some sit-down games to retain this posture. Television is one way but should only be used as the last resort.

5. **Be innovative and occasionally serve your child's meal in plates with different shapes.** For example, a flat plate, a colourful oval shaped plate etc. if she is not attached to one particular plate.

6. **Foods with different shapes and sizes also attract children to eat more.** So it is wise to occasionally serve foods like rotis, biscuits etc in different shapes like round, oval, square etc.

7. **Allow your child to drink milk, soups and juices occasionally with a straw if she wants.** This will take more time but will definitely be a source of motivation for your child to drink more too. Ensure that you wash and clean these straws with sterilised water immediately, since even a little juice or soup left in the straw will harbour germs easily.

8. **If your child shows dislike for a particular ingredient or a food, wait for a few weeks and then try the same one again.** If she reacts in a similar way, do not force her to have that ingredient or food. Instead, try and cook it in a different style.

9. Fried foods and aerated waters are a part of everyone's diet in some form.The trick here is to let them enjoy everything in moderation because the more you forbid them, the more tempting those foods will seem to her. **If you give your child wafers to snack on, ask her to include a fruit in that snack too.** This will make both of you happy.

10. **Avoid using too much salt, sugar and processed and refined products like maida, noodles etc. in your child's daily diet, as much of their goodness has already been destroyed.** They may also contain additional colours, flavourings or preservatives which are unhealthy. Furthermore since the habits you create now will stay with her for a lifetime, it is wiser to stay with whole grains (wheat, bajra, jowar etc.), fruits and vegetables.

11. Kids are usually aware of how much and what they want to eat. **Let the meal end when your little one has had enough.** Do not force, bribe or threaten her to eat more or you might find yourself in a shower of baby food or a resentful little baby.

12. **If your child goes to a day care center, you need to pay extra attention to the food she carried there.** Do not give her perishable foods like curds, soups etc. Instead, give her whole fruits and vegetables like apple, carrot etc. or dry snacks such as biscuits, Cheese Straws, page 112, toast, parathas, chikki, or other foods like Carrot Cake, page 114, Vegetable Idlis, page 95, etc.

49

Tips for Healthy Cooking

Apart from knowing what you can feed your little one, you should also know how to prepare meals in a way that preserves all the nutrients present in those foods. For example, if you're serving juice to your baby, it's much better to make it just before your baby is going to have it, as stored juices lose out on important nutrients like vitamin C which is an unstable and volatile nutrient.

Factors like buying, storing, cooking and serving also influence the nutritional quality of foods.
IT'S IMPORTANT TO:

- ✔ Buy only the freshest fruits and vegetables available in the market. Seasonal fruits are the most nutritious as they ripen without the usage of additional chemicals and are more reasonably priced.
- ✔ Refrigerating food for long period results in the loss of vital nutrients. So buy in small quantities and cook for the day!
- ✔ Washing fruits and vegetables prior to cooking or serving is of utmost importance for the removal of pesticides and other germs present in them.
- ✔ Wash and chop fruits and vegetables just before serving or cooking as this will help to preserve the nutrients and the freshness of these foods.
- ✔ Soaking vegetables in water for a longer period of time will make them lose many valuable water-soluble vitamins like vitamin B and vitamin C.
- ✔ Vegetables should be cooked carefully so that they retain most of their nutrients during the cooking process. Therefore, it is better to sauté or steam vegetables rather than to boil them. If you do boil the vegetables, use minimum quantity of water and cook only until the vegetables become tender. Overcooking them will destroy all the nutrients present in them.
- ✔ Preferably, cover your foods while cooking to preserve the volatile nutrients.
- ✔ Do not throw away the water in which the food has been cooked as it contains water-soluble nutrients such as vitamin B and vitamin C that are released by the vegetables during cooking. Hence, it is advisable to add just enough quantity of water to cover the vegetables while cooking. Any excess cooking water that is remaining can be used to make soups, dals or to knead your chapati dough, as this is a good way to preserve the

water-soluble vitamins.

- ✔ Steaming, sautéing or baking are the best ways to prepare food for your baby as opposed to frying. These methods of cooking help to preserve the nutrient content of foods to a great extent. Vegetable Parathas, page 88, and Spiced Walnut Ring, page 115, are good examples of these healthy cooking methods.

- ✔ The duration of cooking also affects the nutritive value of food served to your baby. The longer the food is cooked, the greater is the loss of heat sensitive nutrients like vitamins B and C. Hence, it is advisable to cook cereals, pulses and vegetables in the minimum possible time, using a pressure cooker, taking care to use the right quantity of water. In case of pulses, it is wiser to soak them ahead of time, so that they cook faster and you do not need to add soda bi-carbonate to speed up the cooking process.

- ✔ Always refrigerate the milk if it has to be stored for a longer period. Do remember to re-heat the frozen milk and then to cool it to room temperature before feeding it to your baby. Check for the quality of the milk by tasting it. Discard the milk if you find it sour.

Hygiene

The health of your little one which is always uppermost in your mind is largely dependent on the hygiene of the environment around her. Initially, babies are totally dependent on breast milk, which is completely safe, after which the transition to top milk takes place. **So, while weaning, it is necessary to maintain hygiene while preparing and serving baby's meals. This is very important as your baby's delicate digestive system has little or no resistance to fight germs, making her very vulnerable to infections.**

I hope that the hints listed below will be of help to you in maintaining an environment that is good for your little one's well being. A hygienic environment is not that difficult to maintain. All it takes is a little thought and pre-planning. Believe me, good hygienic conditions can be maintained with very little effort from your side.

Before you begin cooking or feeding your baby, wash your hands thoroughly preferably with an anti-bacterial soap. It is wiser to wash your baby's hands too both before as well as after meals, as grubby little fists are ideal germ breeders. Also ensure that all the kitchen surfaces have been washed with an anti-bacterial solution and hot water and wiped with a clean cloth before and after cooking. Always use fresh fruits and vegetables that are thoroughly washed with clean water to ensure the removal of pesticides and disease causing germs. **Try to maintain separate cooking utensils as well as feeding spoons and containers for your little one at least till she is 1 year old.** Ensure that all these are properly sterilised before each use. To sterilise them, begin with a liquid soap solution or detergent powder. Scrub carefully and immerse them in boiling water for about half an hour. Remove and dry them with a clean napkin. This kills all the germs, making it safer for your baby. Alternatively, you can also make use of sterilising equipment or a microwave to make the utensils and feeding containers germ free.

If you are using bottles to feed your baby, the chances of contamination increase due to the structure of the bottle. The nipple and the bottom of the bottle are very difficult to clean as a result of which micro-organisms can easily thrive and can affect your baby's digestion. Ensure that the bottle, its nipple and the teat are carefully cleaned before serving it to your baby.

Your baby's drinking water should be boiled thoroughly and then cooled. *Boiling will ensure the destruction of all micro-organisms which can otherwise be harmful to your little one. If you are not sure of the quality of water, double boil it to be safer. Do remember to sterilise the container including the cover completely to prevent contamination.*

Also discard food that has not been consumed within 24 hours, as germs tend to multiply in such foods. If you refrigerate any left-over food, be sure to store it in clean containers and re-heat it thoroughly before serving it.

ABBREVIATIONS USED

The table on the right side lists the abbreviations used in this book.

ABBREVIATIONS

CHO	Carbohydrates
F.ACID	Folic acid
VIT.A	Vitamin A
VIT.C	Vitamin C
AMT	Amount
cm	Centimeters
gm	Grams
kcal	Kilocalories
kg	Kilograms
mcg	Micrograms
mg	Milligrams
ml	Millilitres
IU	International Units

Rice Mash

Rice mash is widely recommended as a great starter to the weaning process. It is easily digestible and is more hygienic than other foods like fruit juices, which are open to chances of contamination due to the several steps involved in preparation. Dilute the rice mash with milk (breast or top) to thin down the consistency so that it is easy for your baby to swallow.

Preparation time : 5 minutes.   Cooking time : 30 minutes.   Makes ½ cup.

2 tablespoons rice
½ teaspoon ghee

1. Wash the rice and add ¾ cup of water. Pressure cook it for 3 whistles.
2. Remove from the pressure cooker and add the ghee. Mix well.
3. Mash it completely to make a smooth consistency. Serve lukewarm.

Nutritive values for ½ cup:

AMT	ENERGY	PROTEIN	CHO	FAT	VIT A	VIT C	CALCIUM	IRON	F.ACID	FIBRE
gm	kcal	gm	gm	gm	mcg	mg	mg	mg	mcg	gm
29	112	1.8	20.3	2.6	22.5	0.0	2.6	0.2	2.1	0.1

Moong Dal Khichdi

This is a good combination of a cereal and a pulse which is suitable for your baby once she has adapted to rice after 1 to 2 weeks of starting weaning. This will add more variety to your baby's meal and also provide plenty of protein for healthy growth.

Preparation time : 15 minutes.   Cooking time : 30 minutes.   Makes ½ cup.

1 tablespoon split green gram (green moong dal)
1 tablespoon rice
½ teaspoon turmeric powder (haldi)
½ teaspoon ghee

1. Wash and soak the green gram and rice together.
2. Add the turmeric powder and pressure cook it for 3 whistles.
3. Remove from the pressure cooker and add the ghee. Mix well.
4. Mash the khichdi completely to make a smooth consistency. Serve lukewarm.

Nutritive values for ½ cup:

AMT	ENERGY	PROTEIN	CHO	FAT	VIT A	VIT C	CALCIUM	IRON	F.ACID	FIBRE
gm	kcal	gm	gm	gm	mcg	mg	mg	mg	mcg	gm
32	123	4.8	19.8	2.8	30.3	0.0	13.3	0.7	23.4	0.2

Moong Dal Water

This is a nourishing food and an ideal one to start with as its texture is similar to that of breast milk. The water has been strained as babies cannot digest whole cereals and pulses before the age of 6 months. It is best to give it unstrained after your little one is 6 months old. To make it tastier, you can add a tadka of ghee, jeera and turmeric powder a couple of weeks after you start this.

Preparation time : 5 minutes.   Cooking time : 15 minutes.   Makes ½ cup.

2 tablespoons yellow moong dal (split yellow gram)

1. Pressure cook the dal in ½ cup of water for 2 whistles.
2. Add an additional ½ cup of water to the cooked dal and liquidise it in a blender.
3. Strain the cooked dal and serve lukewarm.

 You can make even thinner consistency than given above by adding more sterilized water to the dal.

Nutritive values for ½ cup:

AMT	ENERGY	PROTEIN	CHO	FAT	VIT A	VIT C	CALCIUM	IRON	F.ACID	FIBRE
gm	kcal	gm	gm	gm	mcg	mg	mg	mg	mcg	gm
32	111	7.8	19.2	0.4	15.7	0.0	24.0	1.2	44.8	0.3

VARIATION:

Masoor Dal Water

Two tablespoons of masoor dal (split red lentil) can be used instead of moong dal as a variation.

Barley Water

Barley is a protein rich cereal and is very good for your baby when weaning begins. Flavour the barley water with jaggery which is a rich source of iron. Also squeeze some lemon juice into it to provide the much needed vitamin C that protects your baby from coughs and colds.

Preparation time : 5 minutes.   Cooking time : 20 minutes.   Makes 1½ cups

1 tablespoon barley (jav)
2 tablespoons jaggery (gur), grated
1 tablespoon lemon juice

1. Pressure cook the barley with 2 cups of water and the jaggery.
2. Wash, cool and liquidise it in a blender.
3. Strain and allow to cool completely.
4. Add the lemon juice. Mix well and serve lukewarm.

Nutritive values for 1½ cups:

AMT	ENERGY	PROTEIN	CHO	FAT	VIT A	VIT C	CALCIUM	IRON	F.ACID	FIBRE
gm	kcal	gm	gm	gm	mcg	mg	mg	mg	mcg	gm
78	195	1.8	45.9	0.5	1.2	11.7	52.9	1.2	0.0	1.0

Apple Punch

"An apple a day keeps the doctor away". But this is one fruit babies have trouble digesting in its raw form till they are 6 months old. So, apple punch is a wonderful way of introducing apples to your baby's diet. As your little one grows older, apples can be stewed in lesser water to make a purée and served.

Preparation time : 5 minutes. Cooking time : 10 minutes. Makes ¾ cup.

½ cup apple, peeled and grated
1 to 2 teaspoons jaggery (gur), optional

1. Boil ¾ cup of water in a pan. Add it to the apples and jaggery and keep aside for 10 minutes.
2. Strain it to obtain the punch. Serve lukewarm.

Nutritive values for ¾ cup:

AMT	ENERGY	PROTEIN	CHO	FAT	VIT A	VIT C	CALCIUM	IRON	F.ACID	FIBRE
gm	kcal	gm	gm	gm	mcg	mg	mg	mg	mcg	gm
50	49	0.1	11.6	0.2	0.0	0.4	9.2	0.4	0.0	0.4

Papaya and Muskmelon Juice

This unusual combination is an innovative way of introducing a 2 fruit combination in your baby's diet. Rich in vitamin A, vitamin C and fibre, this combination will also help cleanse your baby's digestive system.

Of course, it is always wiser to start off with a single fruit like papaya for a few days and then to introduce the muskmelon for a few days to ensure that your baby is not allergic to either of these fruits.

Preparation time : 10 minutes. No cooking. Makes ½ cup.

½ cup papaya, peeled and chopped
½ cup muskmelon (kharbooja), peeled and chopped

Liquidise both the fruits together in a blender. Strain through a sieve and serve immediately.

Nutritive values for ½ cup:

AMT	ENERGY	PROTEIN	CHO	FAT	VIT A	VIT C	CALCIUM	IRON	F.ACID	FIBRE
gm	kcal	gm	gm	gm	mcg	mg	mg	mg	mcg	gm
145	35	0.6	7.7	0.2	593.0	59.4	35.9	1.4	0.0	0.9

Beetroot and Carrot Soup

I must admit that this is a brightly coloured soup and you're going to have a lot of stained "bibs" initially.

Carrots provide vitamin A which is good for your baby's skin and the beetroot adds sweetness, colour and fibre. Try the other combinations mentioned below as "variety is the spice of life". I have started with a combination of 2 vegetables and then added more vegetables to the soup. Remember to ensure that your baby is not allergic to any of them.

Preparation time : 5 minutes.   Cooking time : 15 minutes.   Makes 1 cup.

¼ cup beetroot, peeled and chopped
½ cup carrot, peeled and chopped

1. Combine the beetroot and carrot in a pressure cooker with 1 cup of water and pressure cook for 2 whistles.
2. Cool and purée into a smooth soup.
3. Strain the soup and re-heat to lukewarm before serving.

Nutritive values for 1 cup:

AMT	ENERGY	PROTEIN	CHO	FAT	VIT A	VIT C	CALCIUM	IRON	F.ACID	FIBRE
gm	kcal	gm	gm	gm	mcg	mg	mg	mg	mcg	gm
47	22	0.6	4.6	0.1	529.2	2.7	25.9	0.5	4.2	0.5

Beetroot, Carrot and Cauliflower Soup

½ cup beetroot, peeled and chopped
¼ cup carrot, peeled and chopped
¼ cup cauliflower, chopped

Bottle Gourd, Cauliflower and Potato Soup

½ cup bottle gourd (doodhi/ lauki), peeled and chopped
¼ cup cauliflower, chopped
¼ cup potato, peeled and chopped

Potato and Vegetable Soup

¼ cup potatoes, peeled and chopped
¼ cup carrots, peeled and chopped
¼ cup french beans, stringed and chopped
¼ cup cauliflower, chopped

Mixed Vegetable Soup

½ cup cauliflower, chopped
½ cup bottle gourd (doodhi/ lauki), peeled and chopped
½ cup carrots, peeled and chopped
¼ cup tomatoes, chopped

 These soups can be served unstrained, once your baby is over the age of 6 months.

Apple and Carrot Soup with Potatoes

This is a slightly more "gourmet" soup.

Rich in energy and vitamin A, this soup is a "solid" meal which will make baby feel satisfied. You will notice that she won't be hungry very quickly after she has "dined" on this one.

As your baby approaches the 6th month, you can start adding ingredients like onions that have a strong flavour to improve the taste. You can add a dash of salt and pepper to this soup after your baby is 6 months old.

Preparation time : 10 minutes.   Cooking time : 15 minutes.   Makes 1¼ cups.

¼ cup apple, peeled and chopped
2 tablespoons carrot, peeled and chopped
¼ cup potato, peeled and chopped
1 tablespoon onion, chopped
½ teaspoon oil

1. Heat the oil in a pressure cooker and sauté the onion for 2 minutes.
2. Add the apple, carrot and potato and sauté for 2 to 3 minutes.
3. Add 1 cup of water and pressure cook for 2 to 3 whistles.
4. Cool and purée in a liquidiser.
5. Strain and re-heat to lukewarm before serving.

Nutritive values for 1¼ cups:

AMT	ENERGY	PROTEIN	CHO	FAT	VIT A	VIT C	CALCIUM	IRON	F.ACID	FIBRE
gm	kcal	gm	gm	gm	mcg	mg	mg	mg	mcg	gm
75	72	0.6	11.3	2.7	254.8	5.1	17.4	0.5	3.7	0.6

Dal Mash

Dal mash is a good supplementary meal to meet your baby's increased demands of energy and proteins. Begin with a simple dal mash and later on add vegetables to it. After 6 months of age, you can add a dash of pepper and a few drops of lemon juice to enhance its flavour.

Preparation time : 10 minutes.   Cooking time : 15 minutes. Makes ½ cup.

2 tablespoons yellow moong dal (split yellow gram)
¼ cup carrot, peeled and chopped
2 to 3 french beans, stringed and finely chopped

1. Pressure cook all the ingredients together with ½ cup of water for 3 whistles.
2. Liquidise the mixture in a blender. Serve lukewarm.

 You can also add crumbled whole wheat flour rotis into the dal mixture and mash it to make a complete meal for your baby after she is 6 months old.

Nutritive values for ½ cup:

AMT	ENERGY	PROTEIN	CHO	FAT	VIT A	VIT C	CALCIUM	IRON	F.ACID	FIBRE
gm	kcal	gm	gm	gm	mcg	mg	mg	mg	mcg	gm
51	119	8.1	20.9	0.4	286.9	1.6	37.7	1.4	49.2	0.5

VARIATION :
Mixed Dal Mash

Substitute the 2 tablespoons of yellow moong dal with 1 tablespoon of yellow moong dal and 1 tablespoon of masoor dal.

Apricot and Fig Purée

Most babies take to figs very enthusiastically because of their mildly sweet taste and grainy texture — something new for their palates. Apricot and fig purée, thinned down with milk, is a good combination rich in vitamin A and fibre. Milk adds calcium which is required for the healthy development of your baby's bones.

Preparation time : 7 to 8 minutes.   No cooking.   Makes ½ cup.

2 dried apricots
2 dried figs
¼ cup milk

1. Soak the apricots and figs in lukewarm water for about half an hour. Drain both the apricots and figs and deseed the apricots.
2. Add the milk and liquidise in a blender to make a smooth purée.
3. Strain to remove the seeds of the figs. Serve immediately.

Nutritive values for ½ cup:

AMT	ENERGY	PROTEIN	CHO	FAT	VIT.A	VIT.C	CALCIUM	IRON	F.ACID	FIBRE
gm	kcal	gm	gm	gm	mcg	mg	mg	mg	mcg	gm
70	76	2.2	7.7	3.0	98.2	1.3	112.3	0.5	2.5	0.5

VARIATIONS:

Banana and Papaya Purée

This delicious purée with 4 tablespoons of banana purée and 4 tablespoons of papaya purée is also healthy for your baby.

Papaya and Mango Purée

Your little one will also relish the combination of ¼ cup of papaya purée mixed with ¼ cup of mango purée and ½ teaspoon of lemon juice.

Mango and Coconut Purée

A purée of ½ cup of chopped mango and ¼ cup of chopped tender coconut flesh can also be occasionally served as a variation. Don't add milk to this combination however.

Banana Smoothie

Bananas are a very baby friendly fruit and one of the very few that babies can eat raw. Bananas when combined with curds and orange juice in this velvety concoction provide your baby with energy, carbohydrates, calcium, vitamin A and vitamin C.

Preparation time : 10 minutes.   No cooking.   Makes ½ cup.

½ cup banana, chopped
1 teaspoon fresh curds (yoghurt)
2 tablespoons orange juice

Combine all the ingredients in a blender and liquidise into a smooth purée. Serve immediately.

 All the ingredients for this drink should be at room temperature.

Nutritive values for ½ cup:

AMT	ENERGY	PROTEIN	CHO	FAT	VIT.A	VIT.C	CALCIUM	IRON	F.ACID	FIBRE
gm	kcal	gm	gm	gm	mcg	mg	mg	mg	.mcg	gm
185	183	2.1	41.6	0.8	129.5	29.8	37.5	0.8	0.3	0.6

Strawberry Yoghurt

This is one of my favourite recipes and I'm sure your baby will love it too. Yoghurt is easier to digest than milk and provides almost the same amount of calcium (which is required to strengthen your baby's bones and teeth). Also strawberry adds to the vitamin C content which is extremely important to protect your baby from coughs and colds.

Try adding mangoes instead of strawberries when they are in season.

Preparation time : 5 minutes.   No cooking.   Makes 1 cup.

5 to 6 ripe strawberries
½ cup fresh thick curds (yoghurt)
sugar to taste (optional)

Liquidise all the ingredients together in a blender and serve immediately.

Nutritive values for 1 cup:

AMT	ENERGY	PROTEIN	CHO	FAT	VIT A	VIT C	CALCIUM	IRON	F.ACID	FIBRE
gm	kcal	gm	gm	gm	mcg	mg	mg	mg	mcg	gm
136	133	4.6	8.5	6.6	166.5	19.7	220.8	0.8	5.6	0.4

Bulgur Wheat Porridge

This wholesome and satisfactory porridge is good for your baby now that she is growing rapidly and her appetite is also increasing. It will keep her satisfied for a couple of hours.

It is a very good source of important nutrients like energy, carbohydrates, calcium, vitamin A and iron. Dates are used to sweeten this porridge as they provide iron and fibre in substantial quantities.

Preparation time : 5 minutes.   Cooking time : 15 minutes.   Makes approx. ½ cup.

1 tablespoon bulgur wheat (dalia)
2 dates (khajur), deseeded
¾ cup milk

1. Pressure cook the bulgur wheat and dates with ½ cup of water for 3 whistles. Cool.
2. Liquidise the cooked bulgur wheat and dates with ½ cup of milk in a blender till it is smooth in texture.
3. Transfer this into a pan and add ¼ cup of water and the remaining ¼ cup of milk and mix well.
4. Bring to a boil, stirring continuously so that no lumps remain. Serve lukewarm.

Nutritive values for ½ cup:

AMT	ENERGY	PROTEIN	CHO	FAT	VIT.A	VIT.C	CALCIUM	IRON	F.ACID	FIBRE
gm	kcal	gm	gm	gm	mcg	mg	mg	mg	mcg	gm
180	287	7.5	33.9	10.0	240.0	1.5	333.8	1.4	8.4	0.2

Bajra Porridge

Occasionally, you can use 1 tablespoon of whole bajra (black millet) as a substitute for 1 tablespoon of bulgur wheat.

Jowar Porridge

You can also add 1 tablespoon of whole jowar (white millet) instead of the bulgur wheat.

Jowar and Ragi Porridge

A combination of cereals like ½ tablespoon of whole jowar (white millet) and ½ tablespoon of whole ragi (nachni) will also be a good alternative. You can also experiment with other combinations like jowar, bajra, ragi etc.

Malted Magic

A great combination of malted cereals and pulses that provides energy, protein and folic acid. Nachni is not a commonly used cereal which is sad because it is extremely rich in iron and calcium as compared to other cereals. You can store this mixture in an air-tight container for a couple of weeks.

Preparation time : 10 minutes.   Cooking time : 25 minutes.   Makes ½ cup.
Soaking time: 6 to 8 hours.

For the malted magic mixture
¼ cup rice, washed and dried
¼ cup whole moong (green gram), raw
¼ cup whole wheat (gehun)
¼ cup whole ragi (nachni)

For serving
1 tablespoon of the mixture
½ cup hot milk
¼ cup mashed banana

For the malted magic mixture

1. Soak the whole moong, whole wheat and ragi in separate containers for 6 to 8 hours.
2. Drain out all the water, tie them in separate muslin cloths and allow them to sprout. This may take upto 2 days in warm weather. Remember to keep sprinkling water on the muslin cloth to keep it damp, as the grains will not sprout if they are dry.
3. Dry roast all the whole grains separately on a tava (griddle) over a slow flame, stirring continuously till they are crisp and can be easily powdered.
4. Cool for 5 minutes and combine all the toasted grains. Rub them between your palms to remove all the burnt skin and sprouts which will otherwise leave a burnt taste in the mixture.
5. Separate this burnt portion from the toasted grains by passing it through a sieve. Discard the burnt portion.
6. Grind the toasted grains to make a fine powder.
7. Cool and store in a sterilized air-tight container. Use as required.

How to proceed

1. Take 1 tablespoon of the dry mixture, add the hot milk and mix well. Cover and keep aside for 5 minutes till it is lukewarm.
2. Add the mashed banana, mix well and serve immediately.

Nutritive values per serving:

AMT	ENERGY	PROTEIN	CHO	FAT	VIT A	VIT C	CALCIUM	IRON	F.ACID	FIBRE
gm	kcal	gm	gm	gm	mcg	mg	mg	mg	mcg	gm
158	191	7.7	35.7	6.9	213.5	5.0	250.7	1.2	9.2	0.8

Instead of bananas you can also use mashed chickoo, puréed dates or jaggery to sweeten this malted mixture.

7 to 9 months

Apple Strawberry Purée

Strawberries are sharper in flavour than other fruits, so use a mild fruit like apple to tone it down. Milk provides calcium and strawberries supplement it with vitamin C which is extremely essential to strengthen your baby's immunity. You can also use bananas instead of apples.

Preparation time : 10 minutes.   No cooking.   Makes ½ cup.

1 cup apples, peeled and chopped
5 to 6 ripe strawberries
2 tablespoons milk

1. Liquidise the apples and strawberries together in a blender.
2. Strain to remove the strawberry seeds.
3. Add the milk, mix well and serve immediately.

Nutritive values for ½ cup:

AMT	ENERGY	PROTEIN	CHO	FAT	VIT.A	VIT.C	CALCIUM	IRON	F.ACID	FIBRE
gm	kcal	gm	gm	gm	mcg	mg	mg	mg	mcg	gm
182	119	1.8	20.6	2.6	54.5	20.2	85.4	1.5	1.7	1.6

Chickoo Milk Shake

Chickoo is another very baby friendly fruit because of its natural sweetness, mild flavour and easy to swallow texture. Most babies relish chickoos and so I have added milk to supplement it with calcium, protein and vitamin A. It is important to remember to remove the pith carefully and to peel off a nice thick layer of the skin, as these portions can hinder your baby's digestion, especially till the age of 1 year.

Preparation time : 5 minutes.   No cooking.   Makes 1 cup.

¼ cup chickoo, peeled, deseeded and chopped
¾ cup milk

Blend the ingredients together in a liquidiser and serve immediately.

68

Nutritive values for 1 cup:

AMT	ENERGY	PROTEIN	CHO	FAT	VIT.A	VIT.C	CALCIUM	IRON	F.ACID	FIBRE
gm	kcal	gm	gm	gm	mcg	mg	mg	mg	mcg	gm
183	208	6.7	14.6	1 0.1	272.0	3.5	324.2	0.7	8.4	0.9

Fruity Phirnee

Creamy and yummy! Another version of rice porridge that's perked up with fruits. The rice flour makes the phirnee creamy and smooth in texture and is great for babies who do not like fruits or milk. This dish is a good source of energy, protein, vitamin A and calcium.

Preparation time : 5 minutes.   Cooking time : 10 minutes.   Makes approx.½ cup.

    1 cup milk
    1½ teaspoons rice flour
    1 tablespoon jaggery (gur), grated
    3 tablespoons fresh fruit purée (strawberry or peach or
    apricot or mango)

1. Bring the milk to a boil in a non-stick pan and add the rice flour.
2. Mix well and simmer till the rice is cooked (7 to 8 minutes).
3. Add the jaggery and mix well till the jaggery dissolves.
4. Cool and add the fruit purée. Serve at room temperature.

 You can also serve the phirnee without fruits, adding a little bit of saffron and cardamom.

Nutritive values for ½ cup:

AMT	ENERGY	PROTEIN	CHO	FAT	VIT.A	VIT.C	CALCIUM	IRON	F.ACID	FIBRE
gm	kcal	gm	gm	gm	mcg	mg	mg	mg	mcg	gm
247	329	9.1	33.0	13.1	324.3	14.5	442.1	1.3	11.6	0.3

Jowar Banana Sheera

After the age of 6 months, your baby will be ready to have foods that are of a more solid consistency. This is just the right dish to start with. It is rich in carbohydrates, protein, iron and calcium and will keep your baby 'full' for a longer period of time. I have used banana to sweeten this sheera to make minimal use of jaggery.

Preparation time : 10 minutes.   Cooking time : 20 minutes.   Makes approx. ¾ cup.

¼ cup jowar flour (white millet flour)
1 teaspoon jaggery (gur), chopped
½ banana, mashed
½ cup milk
1 teaspoon ghee

1. Heat the ghee in a pan and add the jowar flour to it. Sauté till it is light brown in colour.
2. Add the milk and ½ cup of water along with the jaggery, stirring continuously so that no lumps remain.
3. When the sheera is cooked, add the mashed banana and mix well.
4. Serve lukewarm, adding some warm milk to dilute the consistency to suit your baby's requirements.

Nutritive values for ¾ cup:

AMT	ENERGY	PROTEIN	CHO	FAT	VIT.A	VIT.C	CALCIUM	IRON	F.ACID	FIBRE
gm	kcal	gm	gm	gm	mcg	mg	mg	mg	mcg	gm
164	302	7.2	36.0	12.0	238.9	3.0	225.7	1.4	10.4	0.5

Banana Apple Pudding

A fruity meal that all babies will love. This recipe will also encourage your baby to "chew" the food before she swallows it.

Most babies like to chew on biscuits, even if they have no teeth. A biscuit has been included in this recipe to add a little crunch and a taste of familiarity so that they enjoy this pudding more.

Preparation time : 10 minutes.   Cooking time : 15 minutes.   Makes 1 cup.

> ½ cup banana, chopped
> ½ cup apple, peeled and chopped
> 1½ tablespoons brown sugar or jaggery (gur)
> 1 digestive biscuit, crushed
> ½ teaspoon ghee

1. Heat the ghee in a pan and sauté the chopped fruits till they are soft.
2. Add the sugar and mix well till it dissolves.
3. Add the biscuit to the mixture, stir for 2 minutes and serve lukewarm.

Nutritive values for 1 cup:

AMT	ENERGY	PROTEIN	CHO	FAT	VIT.A	VIT.C	CALCIUM	IRON	F.ACID	FIBRE
gm	kcal	gm	gm	gm	mcg	mg	mg	mg	mcg	gm
252	380	2.7	80.7	5.3	139.5	11.1	55.1	1.8	0.0	1.2

Yummy Apple Porridge

This wholesome porridge made of oats, apples and milk can be served as a dessert or breakfast after your baby is 6 months. Milk is a good source of calcium, which is extremely important for the development of your baby's bones and teeth. Oatmeal is high in energy, protein and fibre.

Preparation time : 5 minutes.   Cooking time : 10 minutes.   Makes ½ cup.

> 3 tablespoons quick cooking rolled oats
> ½ cup milk
> 1 tablespoon jaggery (gur), grated
> ¼ apple, peeled and finely chopped
> 1 teaspoon butter

Spinach Pasta Purée

Now that your baby is above the age of 6 months, try this whole wheat pasta purée. The addition of spinach provides iron and folic acid. Paneer makes it all the more delicious and also provides calcium for the healthy growth of your baby's bones. This purée is a good source of vitamin A that is necessary for healthy skin and good vision and of folic acid necessary for normal growth and development of your little one.

If you find that your baby does not like the taste of pepper, avoid adding it to her meals.

Preparation time : 20 minutes.   Cooking time : 25 minutes.   Makes ½ cup.

½ cup spinach (palak), chopped
1½ tablespoons whole wheat pasta (spaghetti, penne, stellini, or any other small pasta)
1 tablespoon paneer (cottage cheese), shredded
salt and pepper to taste

1. Boil 2 cups of water in a pan and add the pasta.
2. Allow it to cook completely. Drain out all the water and keep the pasta aside.
3. Cook the spinach in approx. ½ cup of water and allow it to simmer for 2 to 3 minutes.
4. Add the cooked pasta, paneer, salt and pepper and mix well.
5. Bring it to a boil and cool slightly.
6. Liquidise this mixture in a blender to make a smooth purée. Serve lukewarm.

 Once your baby is older, you can serve this dish without puréeing it.

Nutritive values for ½ cup:

AMT	ENERGY	PROTEIN	CHO	FAT	VIT.A	VIT.C	CALCIUM	IRON	F.ACID	FIBRE
gm	kcal	gm	gm	gm	mcg	mg	mg	mg	mcg	gm
52	68	3.0	7.7	2.7	1933.8	9.8	74.3	0.7	43.2	0.2

Coriander Curd Rice

This mildly flavoured combination of rice with a vegetable (coriander) and a dairy product (curds) helps you to introduce more flavours to your baby's food. It paves the way for her to adapt to the family food more easily later on, when she is about a year old.

This is a great recipe for a hot summer lunch. You can even grate a little bit of carrots or cucumber into this dish as a variation.

Preparation time : 5 minutes.   Cooking time : 15 minutes.   Makes ¾ cup.

2 tablespoons rice, washed
¼ teaspoon cumin seeds (jeera)
a pinch asafoetida (hing)
3 to 4 tablespoons fresh curds (yoghurt)
1 tablespoon chopped coriander
½ teaspoon ghee or oil
salt to taste

1. Heat the ghee in a pan and add the cumin seeds.
2. When the seeds crackle, add the asafoetida and the rice and sauté for 2 to 3 minutes.
3. Add approx. ¾ cup of water and cook till the rice is overdone and can be mashed easily.
4. Cool the rice, add the curds, coriander and salt and blend it slightly to make a rough purée. Serve at room temperature.

Nutritive values for ¾ cup:

AMT	ENERGY	PROTEIN	CHO	FAT	VIT.A	VIT.C	CALCIUM	IRON	F.ACID	FIBRE
gm	kcal	gm	gm	gm	mcg	mg	mg	mg	mcg	gm
85	176	4.1	23.2	6.1	314.8	4.6	119.4	0.3	5.0	0.1

Palak Paneer Rice

This rice delicacy is appealing to most infants because of its bright green colour. Spinach provides the much needed iron and folic acid for your growing baby while paneer is a good source of calcium. This nourishing rice serves as a full meal for lunch or dinner, keeping your baby satiated for a longer time.

Preparation time : 15 minutes.   Cooking time : 15 minutes.   Makes 1 cup.

¼ cup rice
¼ cup spinach (palak), chopped
¼ cup paneer (cottage cheese), chopped
a pinch cumin seeds (jeera)
½ teaspoon ghee or oil
salt to taste

1. Heat the ghee in a pan and add the cumin seeds.
2. When the seeds crackle, add the rice and sauté for 2 to 3 minutes.
3. Add the spinach, paneer, salt and 1 cup of water and pressure cook for 2 to 3 whistles. Mix well and serve lukewarm with fresh curds or dal.

Nutritive values for 1 cup:

AMT	ENERGY	PROTEIN	CHO	FAT	VIT.A	VIT.C	CALCIUM	IRON	F.ACID	FIBRE
gm	kcal	gm	gm	gm	mcg	mg	mg	mg	mcg	gm
98	275	8.1	34.7	11.5	887.0	4.8	195.9	0.4	19.2	0.2

Vegetable Khichdi

Khichdi is a complete meal in itself providing plenty of energy, protein and folic acid to your baby. The addition of carrots makes it rich in vitamin A and fibre. This recipe is a good way of introducing a mildly spiced meal to your baby's diet.

Preparation time : 15 minutes.   Cooking time : 15 minutes.   Makes approx. 1 cup.

2 tablespoons rice
2 tablespoons moong dal (split yellow gram)
1 tablespoon bottle gourd (doodhi/ lauki), peeled and grated
2 tablespoons carrot, peeled and grated
1 peppercorn
1 clove
a pinch turmeric powder (haldi)
¼ teaspoon cumin seeds (jeera)
a pinch asafoetida (hing)
½ teaspoon ghee
salt to taste

1. Wash the rice and moong dal together and keep aside.
2. Heat the ghee in a pressure cooker and add the cumin seeds.
3. When the seeds crackle, add the asafoetida, clove and peppercorn.
4. Add the bottle gourd and carrot and sauté for a few seconds.
5. Add the dal, rice, turmeric powder, salt and 1½ cups of water and pressure cook for 3 whistles.
6. When it is done, remove the peppercorn and clove. Whisk to combine the rice and dal together. Serve lukewarm with fresh curds.

Nutritive values for 1 cup:

AMT	ENERGY	PROTEIN	CHO	FAT	VIT.A	VIT.C	CALCIUM	IRON	F.ACID	FIBRE
gm	kcal	gm	gm	gm	mcg	mg	mg	mg	mcg	gm
89	221	8.8	39.7	3.0	452.0	0.7	43.2	1.5	44.6	0.6

teething foods

Whole Wheat Bread Sticks

Teething is a difficult time for both your baby and you. Baby's gums will feel raw and irritable and she will want to chew on firm or hard things to ease her discomfort.

Crispy whole wheat bread sticks soothe sore gums and also encourage baby to "hold" her food and chew on it.

The whole wheat flour and sesame seeds contribute calcium and iron in your little one's diet. Make a lot of these and store them in an air-tight container.

Preparation time : 1 hour. Baking time : 40 minutes. Makes approx. 32 sticks.
Baking temp. : 140°C (285°F).

¾ cup whole wheat flour (gehun ka atta)
1 tablespoon wheat bran
1 tablespoon sesame seeds (til)
½ teaspoon fresh yeast
½ teaspoon sugar
½ teaspoon salt
1 teaspoon butter

1. Combine all the ingredients except the butter and knead into a soft dough using enough warm water.
2. Add the butter and knead again till the dough is smooth and elastic.
3. Cover with a damp muslin cloth and keep aside for 25 to 30 minutes till the dough proves and is double in volume.
4. Divide the dough into 2 equal parts and roll out each portion into a 100 mm. x 125 mm. (4" x 5") sheet of 6 mm. (¼") thickness.
5. Cut each sheet into 6 mm. (¼") wide strips and separate them. Roll them individually so that they are circular and have no rough edges which can hurt baby's gums.
6. Place them on a greased baking tray and bake in a pre-heated oven at 140°C (285°F) for 40 minutes or till the bread sticks are crisp and golden brown.
7. Cool and store in an air-tight container.

The water should be warm so that the yeast gets activated. If the water is hot, it will kill the yeast instead of activating it.

Nutritive values per bread stick:

AMT	ENERGY	PROTEIN	CHO	FAT	VIT A	VIT C	CALCIUM	IRON	F.ACID	FIBRE
gm	kcal	gm	gm	gm	mcg	mg	mg	mg	mcg	gm
3	12	0.4	2.0	0.3	3.9	0.0	5.9	0.2	1.3	0.1

Jowar Bajra Bread Sticks

This version of bread sticks is more wholesome than the regular bread sticks made from refined flour (maida). It's also an interesting way to introduce different kinds of cereals in your baby's diet.

Preparation time : 1 hour. Baking time : 40 minutes. Makes approx. 32 sticks.
Baking temp. : 140°C (285°F).

¼ cup jowar flour (white millet flour)
¼ cup bajra flour (black millet flour)
¼ cup whole wheat flour (gehun ka atta)
½ teaspoon sugar
1 tablespoon sesame seeds (til)
½ teaspoon fresh yeast
½ teaspoon salt
1 teaspoon butter

1. Combine all the ingredients except the butter and knead into a soft dough using enough warm water.
2. Add the butter and knead again till the dough is smooth and elastic.
3. Cover with a damp muslin cloth and keep aside for 25 to 30 minutes till the dough proves and is double in volume.
4. Divide the dough into 2 equal parts and roll out each portion into a 100 mm. x 125 mm. (4" x 5") sheet of 6 mm. (¼") thickness.
5. Cut each sheet into 6 mm. (¼") wide strips and separate them. Roll them individually so that they are circular and have no rough edges which can hurt baby's gums.

6. Place them on a greased baking tray and bake in a pre-heated oven at 140°C (285°F) for 40 minutes or till the bread sticks are crisp and golden brown.
7. Cool and store in an air-tight container.

Nutritive values per bread stick:

AMT	ENERGY	PROTEIN	CHO	FAT	VIT.A	VIT.C	CALCIUM	IRON	F.ACID	FIBRE
gm	kcal	gm	gm	gm	mcg	mg	mg	mg	mcg	gm
3	11	0.3	1.8	0.3	4.8	0.0	5.4	0.2	0.8	0.1

Teething Biscuits

This is a power-packed recipe!

Soya is an excellent source of vegetarian protein and also provides plenty of vitamin B_{12} that is needed for growing babies.

Chewing on these biscuits will not only comfort your baby's gums but will also provide her with folic acid, fibre, iron, vitamin A and calcium.

I have used ready-made soya flour available at Health Food Stores as I was not happy with the results of the soya flour I made at home using soyabeans.

Preparation time : 5 minutes.   Baking time : 15 minutes.   Makes 18 biscuits.
Baking temp. : 180°C (360°F).

6 tablespoons whole wheat flour (gehun ka atta)
5 tablespoons soya flour
2 tablespoons honey
1 tablespoon oil

1. Combine all the ingredients in a bowl and knead into a dough.
2. Roll out into a 150 mm. x 75 mm. (6" x 3") sheet of 6 mm. (¼") thickness and cut into fingers [50 mm. (2") long and 12 mm. (½") wide].
3. Place the fingers on a greased baking tray and bake in a pre-heated oven for 10 to 12 minutes at 180°C (360°F).
4. When they are cool, store them in an air-tight container.

Nutritive values per biscuit:

AMT	ENERGY	PROTEIN	CHO	FAT	VIT.A	VIT.C	CALCIUM	IRON	F.ACID	FIBRE
gm	kcal	gm	gm	gm	mcg	mg	mg	mg	mcg	gm
9	51	3.1	5.2	2.1	34.4	0.0	17.2	0.8	7.3	0.3

Whole Wheat Date Cookies

Most babies love to nibble on their favourite snack. Biscuits are usually made using refined flour i.e. maida. The use of whole wheat flour in these cookies makes them healthier than other cookies. Also date purée which is used to sweeten these cookies provides iron and fibre.

A great snack to pack when you're taking your baby outdoors for more than an hour or so.

Preparation time : 10 minutes.   Baking time : 25 minutes.   Makes 12 cookies.
Baking temp. : 180°C (360°F).

For the date purée
¼ cup dates (khajur)

For the dough
½ cup whole wheat flour (gehun ka atta)
¼ cup butter
2 tablespoons sugar

For the date purée
1. Chop the dates into small pieces and add ½ cup of water.
2. Bring to a boil in a non-stick pan and simmer for 10 to 12 minutes till the dates are fully mashed into a purée.
3. Cool and keep aside.

For the dough
1. Combine the flour, butter and sugar using your fingertips till the mixture resembles bread crumbs.
2. Add the cooled date purée and knead it into a dough.
3. Cover with a plastic film and refrigerate for 15 minutes.
4. Roll out into a sheet of 6 mm. (¼") thickness and cut out round cookies

approx. 37 mm. (1½") in diameter using a cookie cutter.

5. Re-roll the scraps of dough to make more cookies and place them on a greased baking tray.
6. Bake in a pre-heated oven at 180°C (360°F) for 25 minutes or till the cookies are golden brown.
7. Cool and store in an air-tight container.

Nutritive values per cookie:

AMT	ENERGY	PROTEIN	CHO	FAT	VIT.A	VIT.C	CALCIUM	IRON	F.ACID	FIBRE
gm	kcal	gm	gm	gm	mcg	mg	mg	mg	mcg	gm
14	57	0.6	7.0	2.9	113.3	0.0	3.0	0.3	1.6	0.2

Speckled Bubble Bars

This is another way of introducing your baby to new textures. She may need more variety than carrot strips, crumbly cookies and bread sticks.

The jaggery will keep her energy levels up and also add iron to her diet. The sesame seeds contribute calcium and iron too, while making the process of teething easier.

Preparation time : 5 minutes.   Cooking time : 10 minutes.   Makes 12 bars.

¼ cup jaggery (gur), grated
1 cup puffed rice (mamra), toasted
¼ cup sesame seeds (til), toasted
a pinch cardamom (elaichi) powder (optional)
oil for greasing

1. Melt the jaggery in a heavy bottomed pan over a slow flame until it caramelises.
2. Remove from the fire and add in the rest of the ingredients except the oil. Mix well.
3. Pour this mixture onto a greased marble or stone surface.
4. Using a large greased rolling pin, roll out the praline into a 150 mm. x 112 mm. (6" x 4½") sheet of 12 mm. (½") thickness. (Remember to grease your hands too while rolling this mixture).

5. Cut into 75 mm. x 37 mm. (3" x 1½") bars.
6. Store in an air-tight container.

 You will know the jaggery is caramelised correctly by pouring a drop into a glass of cold water. If it hardens, it is ready. If not, simmer it for a few more minutes. The jaggery should caramelise evenly without burning.

Nutritive values per bar:

AMT	ENERGY	PROTEIN	CHO	FAT	VIT.A	VIT.C	CALCIUM	IRON	F.ACID	FIBRE
gm	kcal	gm	gm	gm	mcg	mg	mg	mg	mcg	gm
7	34	0.6	4.5	1.5	5.3	0.0	39.1	0.4	0.0	0.1

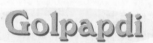

Golpapdi

One of my family favourites, this is a traditional Gujarati sweet dish which has been a hit with babies not only while they were teething but even in later years. Every winter, I still make and store a large batch of golpapdi and usually everyone has one piece in the morning with their breakfast.

It is full of energy, carbohydrates, calcium and iron. The ghee provides large amounts of vitamin A.

Preparation time : 10 minutes. Cooking time : 20 minutes. Makes 24 pieces.

1 cup whole wheat flour (gehun ka atta)
¾ cup jaggery (gur), cut into small pieces
1 teaspoon poppy seeds (khus-khus)
¼ teaspoon cardamom (elaichi) powder
1 teaspoon desiccated coconut (optional)
5 tablespoons ghee, melted

1. Sprinkle the poppy seeds on a 150 mm. (6") diameter greased thali. Keep aside.
2. Melt the ghee in a frying pan and add the wheat flour, stirring continuously till it turns golden brown in colour.
3. Remove from the flame and add the jaggery, cardamom powder and coconut. Stir well.

4. When the jaggery melts and the mixture is still warm, pour it into the greased thali with poppy seeds and spread it evenly with the help of the base of a small bowl (katori).
5. Cut into diamond shapes while still warm.
6. Store in an air-tight container when cool.

Nutritive values per piece:

AMT	ENERGY	PROTEIN	CHO	FAT	VIT.A	VIT.C	CALCIUM	IRON	F.ACID	FIBRE
gm	kcal	gm	gm	gm	mcg	mg	mg	mg	mcg	gm
12	62	0.6	7.7	3.2	29.4	0.0	7.9	0.4	1.6	0.1

10 to 12 months

Jowar and Bajra Rotis with Vegetables

This is an easier way of incorporating a variety of flours and vegetables to your baby's diet between the age of 10 to 12 months. The iron and vitamin A content of this recipe is appreciable due to the addition of fenugreek and carrots. Cooking the rotis with oil or ghee adds on energy content. Serve these rotis with plain curds or raita.

Preparation time : 15 minutes.   Cooking time : 20 minutes.   Makes 4 rotis.

2 tablespoons jowar flour (white millet flour)
2 tablespoons bajra flour (black millet flour)
1 tablespoon fenugreek (methi), chopped
1 tablespoon bottle gourd (doodhi/ lauki), grated
1 tablespoon carrots, grated
¼ teaspoon oil
salt to taste

Other ingredients
4 teaspoons oil or ghee for cooking

1. Combine all the ingredients and knead into a dough using 1 tablespoon of water.
2. Divide the dough into 4 equal portions and roll each portion into 75 mm. (3") diameter circles.
3. Cook each roti on a tava (griddle), using a little oil till it is lightly browned. Serve lukewarm with curds.

Nutritive values per roti:

AMT	ENERGY	PROTEIN	CHO	FAT	VIT.A	VIT.C	CALCIUM	IRON	F.ACID	FIBRE
gm	kcal	gm	gm	gm	mcg	mg	mg	mg	mcg	gm
19	76	0.9	5.6	5.6	124.3	0.5	8.2	0.5	2.9	0.2

Vegetable Parathas

Babies sometimes do not take to vegetables very easily. Vegetable parathas provide a simple way of disguising them in your baby's meals. Carrots and fenugreek leaves make these parathas rich in vitamin A which is extremely important for your baby's healthy vision. Serve these yummy parathas for breakfast at the start of a day or during lunch time.

Preparation time : 20 minutes. Cooking time : 15 minutes. Makes 6 parathas.

½ cup whole wheat flour (gehun ka atta)
1 tablespoon fenugreek (methi) leaves, chopped
1 tablespoon bottle gourd (doodhi/lauki), grated
1 tablespoon carrots, grated
2 tablespoons curds (yoghurt)
a pinch turmeric powder (haldi)
a pinch cumin (jeera) powder
salt to taste

Other ingredients
2 tablespoons ghee for cooking

1. Combine all the ingredients and knead into a dough using enough water.
2. Divide the dough into 6 equal portions and roll each portion into a 75 mm. (3″) diameter circle.
3. Cook each paratha on a tava (griddle), using a little ghee till both sides are lightly browned. Serve lukewarm with curds.

Nutritive values per paratha:

AMT	ENERGY	PROTEIN	CHO	FAT	VIT.A	VIT.C	CALCIUM	IRON	F.ACID	FIBRE
gm	kcal	gm	gm	gm	mcg	mg	mg	mg	mcg	gm
23	83	1.3	6.8	5.5	102.8	0.4	18.6	0.5	3.8	0.2

Bulgur Wheat and Vegetable Khichdi

Khichdi is a complete and wholesome meal in itself, especially when served with curds. This is also a good way to incorporate 2 food groups in one dish i.e. cereals and vegetables. By this time, baby will also begin to "chew" her food and the chopped vegetables in this recipe are a good introduction for that too!

Preparation time : 20 minutes.   Cooking time : 30 minutes. Makes 1 cup.

2 tablespoons bulgur wheat (dalia), washed
2 tablespoons rice, washed
½ small capsicum, chopped
1 tomato, chopped
½ cup spinach (palak), chopped
½ cup cauliflower florets, chopped
⅛ teaspoon turmeric powder (haldi)
⅛ teaspoon cumin seeds (jeera)
a pinch asafoetida (hing)
½ teaspoon ghee
salt and pepper to taste

1. Heat the ghee in a pressure cooker and add the cumin seeds.
2. When they crackle, add the asafoetida, turmeric powder, bulgur wheat, rice and all the vegetables and sauté for 2 to 3 minutes.
3. Add 1½ cups of water, salt and pepper and pressure cook for 3 to 4 whistles till the bulgur wheat is cooked.
4. Mix well and serve lukewarm with curds or raita.

Nutritive values for 1 cup:

AMT	ENERGY	PROTEIN	CHO	FAT	VIT.A	VIT.C	CALCIUM	IRON	F.ACID	FIBRE
gm	kcal	gm	gm	gm	mcg	mg	mg	mg	mcg	gm
232	240	6.5	45.4	3.6	2332.7	92.4	89.0	2.9	67.3	2.0

Dal and Rice with Grated Cabbage

Protein, carbohydrates and fibre are the three important nutrients provided by this recipe. Cabbage adds to the vitamin C content of this delicious dish. This recipe also introduces newer flavours like ginger into your baby's meals. Add a little ginger in the beginning and then gradually increase the quantity as your lil' one gets accustomed to it.

Preparation time : 5 minutes.   Cooking time : 20 minutes.   Makes ¾ cup.

2 tablespoons rice
2 tablespoons moong dal (split yellow gram)
¼ cup cabbage, grated
¼ teaspoon cumin seeds (jeera)
a pinch asafoetida (hing)
¼ teaspoon grated ginger (optional)
a pinch turmeric powder (haldi)
½ teaspoon ghee
salt to taste

For the garnish
1 teaspoon chopped coriander

1. Wash and pressure cook the dal and rice together with 1½ cups of water till the rice and dal are very soft. Keep aside.
2. Heat the ghee in a pan and add the cumin seeds.
3. When the cumin seeds crackle, add the asafoetida and then the ginger.
4. Add the cabbage and sauté for 2 to 3 minutes till it softens.
5. Add the cooked dal, rice, turmeric powder and salt and mix well.
6. Simmer for 4 to 5 minutes. Serve lukewarm garnished with the chopped coriander.

Nutritive values for ¾ cup:

AMT	ENERGY	PROTEIN	CHO	FAT	VIT.A	VIT.C	CALCIUM	IRON	F.ACID	FIBRE
gm	kcal	gm	gm	gm	mcg	mg	mg	mg	mcg	gm
98	221	9.4	39.0	3.0	85.4	50.8	39.6	1.6	50.7	0.7

Bulgur Wheat and Paneer Pulao

Pulao is usually associated with rice. Here, I have tried to make a different kind of pulao using bulgur wheat which has a very good fibre content. Addition of vegetables and paneer makes it all the more nourishing as well as appealing for your infant. Serve it with fresh curds to make a complete meal.

Preparation time : 15 minutes.   Cooking time : 20 minutes.   Makes 1 cup.

2 tablespoons bulgur wheat (dalia), washed
½ teaspoon cumin seeds (jeera)
a pinch asafoetida (hing)
½ cup mixed vegetables (cauliflower, green peas, french beans and carrots), finely chopped
¼ cup paneer (cottage cheese), chopped
1 teaspoon chopped coriander
½ teaspoon lemon juice
½ teaspoon ghee
salt to taste

1. Heat the ghee in a pressure cooker and add the cumin seeds and asafoetida. When the cumin seeds crackle, add the bulgur wheat and sauté for 2 to 3 minutes.
2. Add the vegetables, paneer, 1 cup of water and salt and pressure cook for 3 whistles.
3. Before serving, add the coriander and lemon juice and mix well. Serve lukewarm.

Nutritive values for 1 cup:

AMT	ENERGY	PROTEIN	CHO	FAT	VIT.A	VIT.C	CALCIUM	IRON	F.ACID	FIBRE
gm	kcal	gm	gm	gm	mcg	mg	mg	mg	mcg	gm
139	229	8.0	26.6	10.0	474.5	24.4	189.1	1.9	12.9	1.8

Soya and Vegetable Pulao

A vegetarian diet is deficient in vitamin B_{12} and soya is the only vegetarian food source that is rich in this vitamin. This nourishing pulao has a lot of flavours that will probably be new to your baby. Serve it with curds or dal to mellow down the flavours so that she can adjust to these new additions to her meals.

Preparation time : 5 minutes.   Cooking time : 15 minutes.   Makes 1½ cups.

¼ cup rice, washed
¼ cup soya granules
½ teaspoon cumin seeds (jeera)
a pinch asafoetida (hing)
1 small stick cinnamon (dalchini)
1 green cardamom (elaichi)
¼ cup onions, chopped
¼ cup carrots, peeled and chopped
¼ cup green peas
¼ teaspoon turmeric powder (haldi)
1 teaspoon coriander-cumin seed (dhania-jeera) powder
1 teaspoon ghee
salt to taste

For the garnish
1 tablespoon chopped coriander

1. Boil the soya granules in 1 cup of water till they are soft. Keep aside.
2. Heat the ghee in a pan and add the cumin seeds, cinnamon and cardamom. When the cumin seeds crackle, add the asafoetida and onions and sauté for 2 to 3 minutes.
3. Add the carrots, peas, rice and soya granules and sauté for another 2 minutes.
4. Add the turmeric powder, coriander-cumin seed powder and salt and mix well.
5. Add 1 cup of water and pressure cook for 3 whistles. Mix well.
6. Garnish with the coriander. Serve lukewarm with curds or raita.

If the soya granules are hard to find, use 4 to 5 soya nuggets. Boil them first and then chop them finely.

Nutritive values for 1½ cups:

AMT	ENERGY	PROTEIN	CHO	FAT	VIT.A	VIT.C	CALCIUM	IRON	F.ACID	FIBRE
gm	kcal	gm	gm	gm	mcg	mg	mg	mg	mcg	gm
143	296	11.5	44.9	7.8	601.6	11.3	74.4	2.5	23.4	2.4

Spring Vegetable Risotto

This traditional Italian dish makes a mildly spiced meal for babies who are fond of bland, yet tasty food. The vegetables provide vitamins and fibre while the cheese adds calcium to your baby's diet.

Preparation time : 10 minutes.   Cooking time : 15 minutes.   Makes ½ cup.

2 tablespoons rice, washed
2 tablespoons carrots, grated
1 tablespoon broccoli, chopped
1 tablespoon french beans, chopped
2 tablespoons spring onions, chopped
1 tablespoon onion, chopped
1 clove garlic, grated
1 teaspoon butter
1½ tablespoons cheese, grated
salt to taste

1. Heat the butter in a pan, add the onions and garlic and sauté for 2 to 3 minutes.
2. Add the rice with ¾ cup of water and allow it to cook till the rice is done.
3. Add the carrots, broccoli, spring onions and french beans and cook till the vegetables are soft.
4. Add the cheese and salt and mix well.
5. Mash it to the consistency your baby likes. Serve lukewarm.

Nutritive values for ½ cup:

AMT	ENERGY	PROTEIN	CHO	FAT	VIT.A	VIT.C	CALCIUM	IRON	F.ACID	FIBRE
gm	kcal	gm	gm	gm	mcg	mg	mg	mg	mcg	gm
109	186	6.0	26.9	6.1	838.2	15.6	152.3	1.0	17.9	0.8

Dal and Vegetable Soup

This colourful soup is a good way to combine vegetables and dal, giving your baby fibre, protein and folic acid (from the tomato). Serve it with whole wheat bread sticks and watch your baby dip them into the soup and munch them with relish.

Preparation time : 5 minutes.   Cooking time : 15 minutes. Makes 1 cup.

1 tablespoon moong dal (split yellow gram)
1 tablespoon cow pea (chawli) leaves, chopped
¼ cup tomato, chopped
½ cup cabbage, chopped

1. Wash the dal and combine all the ingredients in a pressure cooker with 1 cup of water.
2. Pressure cook for 2 to 3 whistles.
3. When cool, blend in a liquidiser. Serve lukewarm.

 If cow pea leaves are not available, you can use spinach instead. If your baby likes cheese, you can also add half a slice of cheese to this soup.

Nutritive values for 1 cup:

AMT	ENERGY	PROTEIN	CHO	FAT	VIT.A	VIT.C	CALCIUM	IRON	F.ACID	FIBRE
gm	kcal	gm	gm	gm	mcg	mg	mg	mg	mcg	gm
109	79	5.5	13.4	0.4	983.3	61.9	84.4	3.8	43.5	1.0

Vegetable Idlis

Most babies like the nutty sweetness of coconut and this dish combines coconut beautifully with the fresh flavour of vegetables.

Cut these idlis into strips and let your baby feed herself. This makes a relatively 'safe' food which won't choke baby.

Preparation time : 20 minutes.   Cooking time : 20 minutes.   Makes 10 idlis.
Soaking time : 2 hours.   Fermenting time : 3 to 4 hours.

½ coconut, grated
2 tablespoons urad dal (split black gram)
1 cup parboiled rice
½ onion, finely chopped
½ carrot, grated
¼ cup cabbage, grated
½ teaspoon cumin seeds (jeera)
1 tablespoon grated coconut
salt to taste

Other ingredients
oil for greasing

1. Grind the coconut with 2 cups of warm water in a blender. Strain using a muslin cloth to extract the milk. Keep it aside.
2. Wash and soak the urad dal and parboiled rice together for at least 2 hours.
3. Drain and grind to a fine paste using the coconut milk.
4. Add the onion, carrot, cabbage, cumin seeds, coconut and salt and mix well. Cover and allow to ferment in a warm place for 3 to 4 hours.
5. Pour into greased idli moulds and steam for 10 to 12 minutes.
6. Serve with Corn Sambar, page 96.

Nutritive values per idli:

AMT	ENERGY	PROTEIN	CHO	FAT	VIT.A	VIT.C	CALCIUM	IRON	F.ACID	FIBRE
gm	kcal	gm	gm	gm	mcg	mg	mg	mg	mcg	gm
41	122	2.2	16.6	5.2	102.4	3.3	12.9	0.5	7.8	0.6

Corn Sambar

A quicker version of sambar that's also a variation of the traditional recipe. Grated corn is tempered with mild curry powder. This dish is good with steamed rice or Vegetable Idlis, page 95.

Curry powder is a blend of spices that is available at most grocery stores. While cooking for your baby, choose the mildest variety of curry powder available.

Preparation time : 10 minutes.   Cooking time : 15 minutes.   Makes 1 cup.

¼ cup sweet corn, grated
1 tablespoon onion, chopped
¼ teaspoon cumin seeds (jeera)
a pinch asafoetida (hing)
¼ cup tomato, chopped
½ teaspoon mild curry powder
½ teaspoon ghee
salt to taste

1. Heat the ghee and add the cumin seeds. When they crackle, add the asafoetida.
2. Add the onion and sauté for 2 to 3 minutes.
3. Add the tomato, corn and curry powder and sauté for another 4 to 5 minutes.
4. Add 1 cup of water and bring to a boil.
5. Add salt and simmer for 2 to 3 minutes.
6. Serve lukewarm with Vegetable Idlis, page 95, or steamed rice.

Nutritive values for 1 cup:

AMT	ENERGY	PROTEIN	CHO	FAT	VIT.A	VIT.C	CALCIUM	IRON	F.ACID	FIBRE
gm	kcal	gm	gm	gm	mcg	mg	mg	mg	mcg	gm
120	119	3.6	19.0	3.2	180.5	15.8	30.3	1.0	12.4	0.9

Fruits with Custard

I didn't want to use refined cornflour to make custard, so I experimented with this really easy way to make an instant custard. It's ready in a jiffy and full of goodness too. Serve it with your baby's favourite fruits.

Preparation time : 5 minutes.   Cooking time : 5 minutes.   Makes ¾ cup.

2 tablespoons fresh fruits, chopped

For the custard
½ cup milk
1 digestive biscuit, crushed
1 teaspoon sugar (or jaggery) optional

1. Bring the milk and sugar to a boil and add the biscuit. Allow it to mix with the milk so that the milk thickens. Mix well so that the custard does not have any lumps.
2. Cool completely and add the fruits. Serve immediately.

Nutritive values for ¾ cup:

AMT	ENERGY	PROTEIN	CHO	FAT	VIT.A	VIT.C	CALCIUM	IRON	F.ACID	FIBRE
gm	kcal	gm	gm	gm	mcg	mg	mg	mg	mcg	gm
139	194	5.1	19.0	8.5	413.9	7.9	222.5	0.6	5.6	0.1

over
oneYear

Muskmelon and Watermelon Juice

Most paediatricians advise that children below the age of 1 year should not be given watermelon as it disagrees with their delicate constitution. However, this is a really tasty combination of fruit juices for children over the age of 1 year and your little one is sure to enjoy it.

Preparation time : 10 minutes.   No cooking.   Makes ½ cup.

¼ cup muskmelon (kharbooja), chopped
¼ cup watermelon (tarbuj), chopped

Combine the muskmelon and watermelon and blend in a liquidiser. Serve immediately.

Nutritive values for ½ cup:

AMT	ENERGY	PROTEIN	CHO	FAT	VIT A	VIT C	CALCIUM	IRON	F.ACID	FIBRE
gm	kcal	gm	gm	gm	mcg	mg	mg	mg	mcg	gm
115	19	0.3	3.9	0.2	126.8	19.9	28.4	4.2	0.0	0.4

Plum and Banana Purée

Sharp or acidic fruits like plums are not easily accepted by babies. But these fruits provide plenty of vitamin C and should be included in their diet. Adding some mashed banana tones down the sharpness of the plums and keeps both baby and you happy.

Preparation time : 10 minutes.   No cooking.   Makes 1 cup.

3 ripe plums, peeled and deseeded
1 banana, peeled and deseeded
1 to 2 teaspoons sugar (optional)

Combine all the ingredients, blend in a liquidiser and serve immediately.

Nutritive values for 1 cup:

AMT	ENERGY	PROTEIN	CHO	FAT	VIT.A	VIT.C	CALCIUM	IRON	F.ACID	FIBRE
gm	kcal	gm	gm	gm	mcg	mg	mg	mg	mcg	gm
165	122	1.4	27.5	0.7	223.7	9.4	20.5	0.9	0.0	0.7

Paneer and Vegetable Parathas

Parathas make terrific toddler food since they can usually be enjoyed without parental supervision. Most babies will often hold onto a piece and nibble away while they're busy doing their own thing. They will enjoy these at meal times too with dal and raita.

Preparation time : 10 minutes. Cooking time : 15 minutes. Makes 4 parathas.

For the filling
⅛ cup green peas, boiled and mashed
¼ cup carrots, grated
¼ cup paneer (cottage cheese), grated
2 tablespoons beetroot, grated
1 tablespoon chopped coriander
salt and pepper to taste

For the dough
¾ cup whole wheat flour (gehun ka atta)
1 tablespoon wheat bran
½ teaspoon oil
salt to taste

Other ingredients
4 teaspoons ghee for cooking

For the filling
1. Combine all the ingredients and mix well.
2. Divide into 4 equal portions and keep aside.

100

For the dough
1. Combine all the ingredients in a bowl and knead into a soft dough using enough water.
2. Divide into 4 equal portions and keep aside.

How to proceed
1. Roll out one portion of the dough into a 75 mm. (3") diameter circle.
2. Place a portion of the filling mixture and fold the edges of the dough over the filling.
3. Pinch the edges together to seal the filling in.
4. Flatten the dough and roll out again into a 100 mm. (4") diameter circle.
5. Cook on a tava (griddle) over a medium flame till it is golden brown in colour on both sides, using a little ghee.
6. Repeat for the remaining dough and filling. Serve lukewarm with curds or raita.

Nutritive values per paratha:

AMT	ENERGY	PROTEIN	CHO	FAT	VIT.A	VIT.C	CALCIUM	IRON	F.ACID	FIBRE
gm	kcal	gm	gm	gm	mcg	mg	mg	mg	mcg	gm
51	161	4.4	17.3	8.2	250.8	2.3	64.2	1.4	11.7	0.8

Jowar Bajra Rotis with Paneer

This recipe is a delicious way to introduce a combination of cereals like jowar and bajra flour which are richer in iron and fibre than wheat flour.

Also, the greater the variety of foods babies are introduced to during the first year, the more likely they are to accept newer tastes as adults.

Preparation time: 10 minutes.   Cooking time: 15 minutes.   Makes 4 rotis.

2 tablespoons jowar flour (white millet flour)
2 tablespoons bajra flour (black millet flour)
1 tablespoon paneer (cottage cheese), grated
4 tablespoons spinach (palak), chopped
4 teaspoons ghee or oil to cook

101

1. Combine all the ingredients and knead into a soft dough using water.
2. Divide the dough into 4 equal parts and roll out each part into a 100 mm. (4") diameter circle.
3. Cook each roti on a non-stick tava (griddle) over a medium flame using a little ghee till both sides are golden brown in colour. Serve lukewarm with fresh curds or raita.

Nutritive values per roti:

AMT	ENERGY	PROTEIN	CHO	FAT	VIT.A	VIT.C	CALCIUM	IRON	F.ACID	FIBRE
gm	kcal	gm	gm	gm	mcg	mg	mg	mg	mcg	gm
28	82	1.4	5.8	5.9	786.5	3.7	24.0	0.6	18.5	0.2

Sprouts Khichdi

This yummy khichdi made with sprouted moong has a hint of subtle spices like onions and garlic. If your baby enjoys these, it will ensure that meal times are splatter free and more enjoyable. Fresh curds make a perfect accompaniment for this khichdi.

Preparation time : 10 minutes.   Cooking time : 15 minutes.   Makes 1 cup.

2 tablespoons rice, washed
2 tablespoons sprouts (moong or matki)
1 teaspoon onion, chopped
1 small clove garlic, chopped
¼ teaspoon cumin seeds (jeera)
½ teaspoon ghee
a pinch asafoetida (hing)
salt to taste

1. Heat the ghee in a pan and add the cumin seeds. When they crackle, add the asafoetida and garlic and sauté for a few seconds.
2. Add the chopped onion and salt and sauté again for 2 to 3 minutes.
3. Add the rice, sprouts and ¾ cup of water and pressure cook for 3 whistles.
4. Coarsely mash the khichdi and serve lukewarm with fresh curds or raita.

Nutritive values for 1 cup:

AMT	ENERGY	PROTEIN	CHO	FAT	VIT.A	VIT.C	CALCIUM	IRON	F.ACID	FIBRE
gm	kcal	gm	gm	gm	mcg	mg	mg	mg	mcg	gm
60	139	3.6	25.0	2.7	29.6	0.3	13.4	0.5	2.3	0.4

Beetroot and Carrot Raita

At least 2 glasses of milk per day is essential for toddlers as they require it for the development of bones and teeth. If your toddler is not happy about having milk, try other forms of milk like cheese, curds, paneer etc.
This tongue tickling raita will go well with a paratha or a pulao.

Preparation time : 10 minutes.   No cooking.   Makes ½ cup.

¼ cup fresh curds (yoghurt)
1 tablespoon carrots, peeled and grated
1 tablespoon beetroot, peeled and grated
¼ teaspoon roasted cumin seeds (jeera)
salt to taste
a pinch sugar (optional)

Combine all the ingredients in a bowl and serve immediately.

Nutritive values for ½ cup:

AMT	ENERGY	PROTEIN	CHO	FAT	VIT.A	VIT.C	CALCIUM	IRON	F.ACID	FIBRE
gm	kcal	gm	gm	gm	mcg	mg	mg	mg	mcg	gm
69	61	2.2	4.1	3.0	279.9	1.6	104.8	0.3	4.2	0.2

Fruity Chana Salad

Salads have great nutritive value and should be a part of your baby's meals. While most little ones are not enthusiastic about salads, if you include a few of their preferred ingredients, they won't even notice they're eating salad. You can add any seasonal fruits that are your baby's favourite instead of pomegranate and oranges.

Preparation time : 10 minutes.   Cooking time : 20 minutes.   Makes 1 cup.

¼ cup chick peas (kabuli chana), soaked overnight
¼ cup cucumber, peeled and chopped
1 tablespoon seedless grapes, halved
¼ cup orange segments, peeled and deseeded
black salt (sanchal) to taste

1. Drain out the water from the soaked chick peas.
2. Add fresh water and salt and pressure cook till the chick peas are soft.
3. Drain and cool completely.
4. Combine with all the other ingredients in a bowl and mix well.
   Serve immediately.

Nutritive values for 1 cup:

AMT	ENERGY	PROTEIN	CHO	FAT	VIT.A	VIT.C	CALCIUM	IRON	F.ACID	FIBRE
gm	kcal	gm	gm	gm	mcg	mg	mg	mg	mcg	gm
103	106	4.1	19.5	1.3	525.5	16.1	58.4	1.3	43.6	1.3

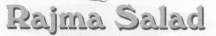

Rajma Salad

This is probably an adventurous salad for toddlers, but I discovered that they like to eat chat-pata food even at this age. Just avoid chillies like I have done in this recipe.
This salad is good for take away lunches too.

Preparation time : 10 minutes.   Cooking time : 20 minutes.   Makes 1 cup.

¼ cup kidney beans (rajma), soaked overnight
¼ cup cucumber, finely chopped
¼ cup tomato, chopped

1 teaspoon lemon juice
½ teaspoon roasted cumin (jeera) powder
salt to taste

1. Drain out the water from the soaked rajma.
2. Add fresh water and salt and pressure cook the rajma until soft. Drain and cool completely.
3. In a bowl, combine with the cucumber, tomato, lemon juice, cumin powder and salt and mix well. Serve immediately.

 If you wish, you can also mash the rajma slightly to make it easier for your toddler to eat.

Nutritive values for 1 cup:

AMT	ENERGY	PROTEIN	CHO	FAT	VIT.A	VIT.C	CALCIUM	IRON	F.ACID	FIBRE
gm	kcal	gm	gm	gm	mcg	mg	mg	mg	mcg	gm
124	150	9.3	26.5	0.7	136.9	17.0	128.2	2.4	17.1	2.5

Soya ki Subzi

This mildly spiced and nutritious subzi will make an excellent accompaniment for rotis and parathas. Soya is "the king of beans" as it is a valuable source of energy, proteins, calcium, iron and fibre, all of which are extremely important for your child's healthy growth. Vegetables like tomato, capsicum, coriander add to the colour and flavour of the subzi making it more appealing for your toddler.

Preparation time : 10 minutes. Cooking time : 20 minutes. Makes 1½ cups.

½ cup soya nuggets
½ teaspoon cumin seeds (jeera)
½ teaspoon ginger, grated
1 small clove garlic, chopped
¼ cup onions, chopped
1 tablespoon capsicum, finely chopped
2 tablespoons cauliflower florets, finely chopped
2 tablespoons carrots, peeled and finely chopped
½ cup tomato, grated

¼ teaspoon turmeric powder (haldi)
1 teaspoon coriander-cumin seeds (dhania-jeera) powder
2 tablespoons milk
1 teaspoon oil
salt to taste

For the garnish
1 tablespoon chopped coriander

1. Boil the soya nuggets in 1½ cups of water till they are soft. Chop into small pieces.
2. Heat the oil and add the cumin seeds. When the cumin seeds crackle, add the onions, ginger, garlic and capsicum and sauté for 2 to 3 minutes.
3. Add the cauliflower and carrots and sauté for another 4 to 5 minutes till the cauliflower is tender.
4. Add the tomato, turmeric powder, coriander-cumin seeds powder andsalt.
5. Mix well and sauté till the oil separates from the gravy. Add the chopped soya nuggets, the milk and 2 tablespoons of water and simmer for 4 to 5 minutes.
6. Garnish with the coriander and serve lukewarm with chapatis or rice.

Nutritive values for 1½ cups:

AMT	ENERGY	PROTEIN	CHO	FAT	VIT.A	VIT.C	CALCIUM	IRON	F.ACID	FIBRE
gm	kcal	gm	gm	gm	mcg	mg	mg	mg	mcg	gm
242	298	20.2	19.1	14.9	1025.7	59.3	233.8	5.3	67.9	2.9

Corn and Peas with Cottage Cheese

Yellow pearls of corn combined with peas and cubes of cottage cheese look really appealing and I'm sure your little angel will enjoy munching on them.

A new flavour of mixed dried herbs is added to perk up this dish, as children at this age do enjoy experimenting with newer flavours.

You should cook both the **peas** and the corn till they are very soft and can be mashed and chewed by your toddler.

Preparation time : 5 minutes. Cooking time : 15 minutes. Makes ¾ cup.

¼ cup sweet corn kernels
¼ cup green peas
¼ cup paneer (cottage cheese), cubed
1 tablespoon onion, chopped
1 clove garlic, chopped
¼ teaspoon mixed herbs (oregano, thyme etc.)
1 teaspoon butter
salt to taste

1. Heat the butter and sauté the onion and garlic for 2 minutes.
2. Add the corn, peas and ½ cup of water and allow to simmer till the peas and corn are soft.
3. Add the paneer, mixed herbs and salt and mix well.
4. Using a fork, mash the corn kernels and peas so that your toddler will not have trouble swallowing them.

Nutritive values for ¾ cup:

AMT	ENERGY	PROTEIN	CHO	FAT	VIT.A	VIT.C	CALCIUM	IRON	F.ACID	FIBRE
gm	kcal	gm	gm	gm	mcg	mg	mg	mg	mcg	gm
130	204	8.8	20.3	9.8	253.6	8.0	166.6	1.2	3.9	1.8

Moong Sprouts Dosa

I am sure your little one will relish this stuffed dosa both as a snack and at meal time. The stuffing is an ideal way of introducing a combination of vegetables to your child's meal. The vegetables not only serve as an important source of nutrients like calcium, iron, vitamin A and fibre, but also give a feeling of fullness and satiate your child for longer periods of time.

I've used sprouts here instead of soaked moong because sprouts are easier to digest and also sprouting increases the nutritive value of pulses.

Preparation time : 20 minutes.   Cooking time : 20 minutes. Makes 4 dosas.

For the dosas
1 cup moong sprouts
4 tablespoons rice flour (chawal ka atta)
salt to taste

For the filling
½ potato, boiled and mashed
2 tablespoons carrot, grated
2 tablespoons beetroot, grated
2 tablespoons cabbage, grated
2 tablespoons chopped onion
¼ cup tomato, finely chopped
1 tablespoon chopped coriander
1 tablespoon fresh coconut, grated
½ teaspoon chaat masala
¼ teaspoon mustard seeds (rai)
2 curry leaves
a pinch turmeric powder (haldi)
a pinch asafoetida (hing)
1 teaspoon oil
salt to taste

Other ingredients
4 teaspoons oil to cook the dosas

For the dosas
1. Combine the sprouts with ¾ cup of water in a blender and grind into a smooth paste.

2. Add the rice flour and salt and mix well so that no lumps remain. Allow the batter to stand for 15 minutes. Add more water if required to adjust the consistency of the batter so that it is of dropping consistency.

For the filling
1. Heat the oil in a pan and add the mustard seeds, curry leaves and turmeric powder.
2. When the mustard seeds crackle, add the asafoetida. Add all the vegetables, fresh coconut and chaat masala to the tempering and mix well.
3. Divide the filling mixture into 4 equal portions. Keep aside.

How to proceed
1. Heat and grease a non-stick tava (griddle) with a little oil.
2. Pour a ladleful of the batter on the tava and spread it evenly using a circular motion.
3. Drizzle a little oil on the sides to allow it to cook.
4. Top with one portion of the filling mixture and spread it evenly over the dosa.
5. When the lower side of the dosa is lightly browned, fold over.
6. Repeat to make 3 more dosas. Serve lukewarm with coconut chutney.

Nutritive values per dosa:

AMT	ENERGY	PROTEIN	CHO	FAT	VIT.A	VIT.C	CALCIUM	IRON	F.ACID	FIBRE
gm	kcal	gm	gm	gm	mcg	mg	mg	mg	mcg	gm
74	172	5.1	20.7	7.7	269.4	12.6	37.8	1.1	6.9	1.1

foods
on the
go

Whole Wheat Bread

Most children love to nibble on bread for a snack. Though it is easily available in the market, it is fun to make your own healthy version using whole wheat flour, when time permits.

For a more nourishing snack make a sandwich using fresh vegetables.

Preparation time : 60 minutes. Baking time : 25 minutes.   Makes 13 slices.
Baking temp. : 200°C (400°F) for 10 minutes.
150°C (300°F) for 15 minutes.

2¼ cups (250 grams) whole wheat flour (gehun ka atta)
2 teaspoons (10 grams) fresh yeast
¾ teaspoon sugar
1 teaspoon butter
¾ teaspoon salt

1. Sieve the flour. Make a well in the centre.
2. Add the yeast, sugar and a little warm water.
3. Wait for at least 4 to 5 minutes or until bubbles surface. Add the butter and salt.
4. Knead into a soft dough by adding some more warm water.
5. Knead well till the dough is smooth and elastic.
6. Cover with a damp muslin cloth and allow it to prove till it doubles in volume (approx. 20 minutes).
7. Knead again, shape into a loaf and place it in a greased loaf tin.
8. Cover with a damp muslin cloth and allow it to prove again till it doubles in volume.
9. Sprinkle some water over the loaf tin and bake in a pre-heated oven at 200°C (400°F) for 10 minutes. Then reduce the temperature to 150°C (300°F) and bake for another 15 minutes.
10. Cool and cut into slices. Use as required.

Nutritive values per slice:

AMT	ENERGY	PROTEIN	CHO	FAT	VIT.A	VIT.C	CALCIUM	IRON	F.ACID	FIBRE
gm	kcal	gm	gm	gm	mcg	mg	mg	mg	mcg	gm
21	69	2.4	13.7	0.5	13.0	0.0	9.3	1.0	6.9	0.4

Cheese Straws

Laden with energy, protein and calcium, these straws will serve as a perfect snack in between meals for your child. Your toddler will love these straws because of their crispy and crunchy texture, which also enhances the chewing ability of your little one.

Preparation time : 15 minutes.   Baking time : 20 minutes. Makes 35 straws.
Baking temp. : 200°C (400°F).

1 cup whole wheat flour (gehun ka atta)
⅓ cup butter
4 tablespoons cheese, grated
2 pinches salt

1. Sieve the flour and add the salt.
2. Rub the butter into the flour with your fingertips till the mixture resembles bread crumbs.
3. Add the cheese and mix well.
4. Add ice-cold water (approx. 1 tablespoon) and make a dough.
5. Roll out the dough on a lightly floured board to about 6 mm. (¼") thickness.
6. Cut into 50 mm. (2") long strips using a knife.
7. Arrange the straws on an ungreased baking tray and bake in a pre-heated oven at 200°C (400°F) for 10 to 12 minutes.
8. Cool completely and store in an air-tight container.

Nutritive values per straw:

AMT	ENERGY	PROTEIN	CHO	FAT	VIT.A	VIT.C	CALCIUM	IRON	F.ACID	FIBRE
gm	kcal	gm	gm	gm	mcg	mg	mg	mg	mcg	gm
6	26	0.6	2.2	1.6	54.0	0.0	9.6	0.2	1.1	0.1

Cheesy Corn and Vegetable Cutlets

These vegetable laden, colourful and mouth watering cutlets are great to tempt the tummy of children with a less predictable palate or a smaller appetite. For more baby friendly appeal, roll the cutlets in fancy shapes and sizes. Serve them as a snack with your child's favourite sauce or sweet chutney, or make a burger or frankie filling with it.

Preparation time : 15 minutes.   Cooking time : 25 minutes.   Makes 6 cutlets.

¼ cup potato, boiled and mashed
¼ cup grated corn
¼ cup carrots, grated
¼ cup cabbage, grated
1 clove garlic, grated
2 tablespoons cheese, grated
1 teaspoon butter
salt to taste

Other ingredients
2 tablespoons oil for cooking

1. Heat the butter, add the corn, carrots, cabbage and garlic and sauté for 4 to 5 minutes. Remove from the flame.
2. Combine the potato, cheese, cooked vegetable mixture and salt and mix well.
3. Divide this mixture into 6 equal portions and shape into small cutlets.
4. Shallow fry on a non-stick pan using a little oil.

Nutritive values per cutlet:

AMT	ENERGY	PROTEIN	CHO	FAT	VIT.A	VIT.C	CALCIUM	IRON	F.ACID	FIBRE
gm	kcal	gm	gm	gm	mcg	mg	mg	mg	mcg	gm
33	81	1.4	4.8	6.3	147.6	6.1	29.6	0.3	1.8	0.2

Carrot Cake

Older children enjoy cake as an occasional treat but plain sponge cakes can be a little boring for them. Carrots have been added as they add variety and also provide substantial amounts of vitamin A and fibre. Cinnamon, nutmeg, honey and jaggery impart delicious flavours to this cake.

This cake is really a great "tiffin box" item that your baby will enjoy during play time.

Preparation time : 15 minutes. Baking time : 1 hour. Makes 24 pieces.
Baking temp. : 180°C (360°F).

1½ cups whole wheat flour (gehun ka atta)
1 teaspoon cinnamon powder (dalchini)
½ teaspoon nutmeg powder (jaiphal)
½ teaspoon baking powder
½ cup butter
⅔ cup honey
½ cup jaggery (gur), grated
2 cups carrots, grated

1. Melt the butter, honey and jaggery over a low flame. Keep aside.
2. Sift the flour with the cinnamon, nutmeg and baking powders.
3. Combine the butter mixture, flour mixture and grated carrots and pour into a greased 200 mm. x 100 mm. (8" x 4") baking pan.
4. Bake in a pre-heated oven at 180°C (360°F) for 1 hour. Cool on a wire rack.

Nutritive values per piece:

AMT	ENERGY	PROTEIN	CHO	FAT	VIT.A	VIT.C	CALCIUM	IRON	F.ACID	FIBRE
gm	kcal	gm	gm	gm	mcg	mg	mg	mg	mcg	gm
29	89	1.1	15.3	3.0	252.6	0.3	15.8	0.5	3.8	0.3

Spiced Walnut Ring

I am sure this spicy cake which is rich in energy, protein and calcium will not fail to please your child. Ginger adds to the flavour as well as helps to ease the digestion of your precious little one. It is also a good snack to take if you are travelling as it keeps well for a few days.

This is a rich recipe and one can indulge in it occasionally. It is good for a toddler who is fussy about food.

Preparation time : 10 minutes.   Baking time : 30 minutes.   Makes 8 pieces.
Baking temp. : 180°C (360°F).

1 cup whole wheat flour (gehun ka atta)
½ teaspoon baking powder
¼ teaspoon ginger powder (soonth)
¼ teaspoon nutmeg powder (jaiphal)
½ teaspoon cinnamon powder (dalchini)
½ cup butter, softened
¼ cup brown sugar
¼ cup condensed milk
⅓ cup milk
¼ cup walnuts, chopped

1. Sieve the flour with the baking powder, ginger powder, nutmeg powder and cinnamon powder.
2. Cream the butter and brown sugar in a bowl till light and fluffy.
3. Add the condensed milk, flour mixture, milk and walnuts and mix well.
4. Pour this mixture into a greased 125 mm. (5") diameter ring mould or a square [150 mm. x 150 mm. (6" x 6")] tin.
5. Bake in a pre-heated oven at 180°C (360°F) for 25 to 30 minutes or until a knife inserted into the cake comes out clean.

Nutritive values per piece:

AMT	ENERGY	PROTEIN	CHO	FAT	VIT.A	VIT.C	CALCIUM	IRON	F.ACID	FIBRE
gm	kcal	gm	gm	gm	mcg	mg	mg	mg	mcg	gm
54	208	3.4	20.1	12.4	377.9	0.4	64.3	0.8	6.6	0.3

Sesame Brittle

Everyone loves crisps and toddlers are no exception to it. Til chikki is particularly irresistible because of its texture and flavour. Til and jaggery both make the chikki highly rich in iron. This chikki is also a good way of encouraging independence in your child as she will learn to hold it and chew it on her own.

Preparation time : 10 minutes.   Cooking time : 10 minutes.   Makes 10 pieces.

½ cup sesame seeds (til), roasted
⅓ cup jaggery (gur), grated
½ teaspoon ghee

Other ingredients
½ teaspoon ghee for greasing

1. Grease the back of a flat thali with ghee and keep it aside.
2. Heat the ghee in a pan and add the jaggery to it. Simmer till it forms a hard ball when it is dropped in water.
3. Add the roasted til and mix thoroughly.
4. When the mixture is ready, pour it over the greased thali. Roll it into a thin layer using a greased rolling pin. (Remember to grease your hands too).
5. Cut into square pieces when it is still warm. Cool completely.
6. Store in an air-tight container.

Nutritive values per piece:

AMT	ENERGY	PROTEIN	CHO	FAT	VIT.A	VIT.C	CALCIUM	IRON	F.ACID	FIBRE
gm	kcal	gm	gm	gm	mcg	mg	mg	mg	mcg	gm
11	55	1.1	6.3	2.9	5.9	0.0	91.0	0.7	0.0	0.2

VARIATION

Peanut Brittle

You can use ½ cup roasted and coarsely powdered peanuts instead of sesame seeds as a variation.

125 @